AN IDYL OF WORK.

BY

LUCY LARCOM.

BOSTON:
JAMES R. OSGOOD AND COMPANY,
LATE TICKNOR & FIELDS, AND FIELDS, OSGOOD, & CO.
1875.

University Press: Welch, Bigelow, & Co.,
Cambridge.

TO WORKING-WOMEN,

This Book

IS DEDICATED

BY ONE OF THEIR SISTERHOOD.

PREFACE.

Some explanation of the intention of this book is perhaps desirable.

It refers to a period in the history of a well-known manufacturing city, about thirty years since, when the work of the mills was done almost entirely by young girls from various parts of New England,—many of whom had comfortable homes, yet chose this method of winning for themselves a degree of pecuniary independence.

The writer of these pages was at an early age familiar with the details of mill-labor; and her first literary efforts were made as a contributor to original magazines like the "Lowell Offering," which were filled, and, for the greater part of their existence, edited, by mill-girls.

A truthful sketch of factory-life, drawn from the memory of it as then known, — and a sketch only, for this "Idyl" does not claim completeness either as poem or as narrative, — is all that she has sought to produce. The routine of such a life is essentially prosaic; and the introduction of several leading characters of equal interest has seemed to make artistic unity impossible: it has not, indeed, been attempted.

And it may be as well to say that, while this is intended to be a truthful sketch, so far as modes of living and working are concerned, and also in touches of character and in some incidents, no one's story herein outlined is that of any particular person the writer has ever known.

In naming the book an "Idyl," it was felt that some play of fancy could be permitted, and the necessarily literal description of work-day occupations relieved by glimpses of the mountain landscapes among which so many of these young working-girls were bred, and to which their thoughts, as well as their feet, would often be found returning. The picturesque beauty of the Merrimack, then almost undisturbed, and the grand background of the New Hampshire hills, whence it descends, do indeed make the memory of those days idyllic.

No one can feel more gratefully the charm of noble scenery, or the refreshment of escape into the unspoiled solitudes of nature, than the laborer at some close in-door employment. The toiler is saved from being a drudge by remembering that his work goes on side by side with the grand processes of creation ; by feeling himself surrounded with the glory of the earth and the heavens, — at once an infolding and a release, — and by entering into great thoughts and hallowed aspirations, as the atmosphere in which it is his right to breathe.

The conditions and character of mill-labor are no doubt much changed since the period indicated ; but the spirit of our national life remains the same. That any work by which mankind is benefited can degrade the worker seems an absurd idea to be met with in a Christian republic, and whatever shadow of it lingers among us is due to the influence of that feudal half-civilization from which we have only partially emerged, and to which, through a morbid desire for wealth, show, and luxury, we are in danger of returning.

Labor, in itself, is neither elevating nor otherwise. It is the laborer's privilege to ennoble his work by the aim with which he undertakes it, and by the enthusiasm and faithfulness he puts into it.

In our country low associations and sacrifice of refinement are no necessities of the toiler's lot. Community of useful interests, in developing the stronger traits of character, gives depth to the attachments of friendship, and intensity to its higher sympathies.

Any needed industry, thoughtfully pursued, brings the laborer into harmony with the unceasing activities of the universe, and yet more closely into unison with the life of loving effort and self-sacrifice revealed through that Divine Person who has taught the race its noblest lessons of ministry and service.

AN IDYL OF WORK.

I.

IN latter April, earth one bud and leaf,
Three girls looked downward from their window-perch:
Three maidens in their different maiden-bloom;
Three buds in their rough calyxes, — for sweet
And rosebud-like is girlhood everywhere;
In culture or wild freedom, lovely still
With promises of all the undawned years.

Three damsels at a casement in old time,
In some high castle-turret, where they wrought
Tapestry for royal mistresses, had been
A picture for a painter, or a theme
For a stray minstrel: full as worthy these.

Under the open window where they stood
A river ran; green farm-lands lay beyond,
And forests, dark against the dreamy hills:

A river less romantic than the Rhine,
Yet fringed with its unwritten histories, —
New England's beautiful blue Merrimack.
And they were idle as queens' ladies now, —
Three girls in their work-aprons, gazing out
Upon the swirling freshet; for the stream
Had risen to a flood, and made the factory-wheels
Drag slow, and slower, till they almost stopped.
The spindle scarcely turned, the thread ran slack,
And lazily the shuttle crossed the web.
Slight watching their work needed; so they stood
And gave free voice to thoughts and fantasies
That groaning shaft and ceaseless clattering loom
Were wont to clamor down.
The room was dim
With April's rainy light, that here and there
Came in through greenery of geranium leaves
Grown lush and fragrant to the window-tops,
Bringing a hint of gardens and thick woods.
The light leaf-shadowings stole tenderly
Over those three girl-figures in their nook, —
Esther, and Eleanor, and Isabel.

Esther was tall and strong, with gold-brown hair
That rippled sunshine to her feet, almost,

When she undid its coil; and sunny light
Seemed ever to stream outward from her mind,
Large, fair, well ordered. Elder-sister-like
Was she to Eleanor and Isabel,
A little while ago two stranger-girls
Adrift in this new city, seeking work;
A mother to the orphan Eleanor,
Whose only heirloom from rich ancestors
Was slow consumption, hers by sure entail.

"Isabel," — it was Eleanor who spoke, —
"You should have been a lady! Every turn
Of shoulder, every poise of arm or foot,
Reminds me of the graceful dames who stooped
To pet me at my father's festivals.
I never see you in that working-gown
And coarse stuff apron, but I find myself
Murmuring 'There's Cinderella!'"

"Where's the shoe?
O for a fairy-coach, a godmother!"
Laughed Isabel; "for I, in honest truth,
Have also dreamed of these things."

"And the prince?"
Asked Esther. Why did foolish Isabel blush?

"Perhaps I am a lady, Eleanor,"
She said, in haste, the sunset of her cheek
Fading along its oval, brown and rich,
And dying in deep dimples. "'Now sit still
And be a little lady, Isabel!'
My mother used to say, when company
Came to take tea with us, and she had fears
That I should be too much myself. And I,
Who had a lady painted on my brain
From English story-books, with folded hands
And puckered lips, sat picturing myself
Some proud earl's daughter. 'Lady!' Who defines
That word correctly?"
"Who defines what word?
Ask me, young woman."
And a gay moon-face,
With laughter pencillings about the eyes,
Round as two moons, and tresses crinkling brown
Over a forehead smooth as infancy's,
Shone in between the looms.
"Well, tell us, then,
What 'lady' means: for, Minta Summerfield,
They say I'm like one; not the real thing!"

"Not know what 'lady' means, young Isabel,
Seeing me straight before you? Esther Hale,

The Lady Isabel doubts Lady Me!
I 've heard you called a walking dictionary, —
Enlighten us, please!"
"'Lady' or 'girl' or 'woman,'
Whichever word you choose," said Esther, "each
Means excellence and sweetness. 'Lady,' though,
Can slip its true sense, leaving an outside
Easy to imitate. At first it meant
'Giver of loaves.' I 've heard it rhymed, this way:—

THE LOAF-GIVER.

"Is there a lady yet
  Under the sun?"
Dames of Olympus
  Called down, one by one.

"If a true lady
  Be left, of earth's race,
Seats of the goddesses
  Offer her place."

Answer came slowly
  From hemispheres two:
Dead seemed the Old World,
  And heedless the New.

"I am a lady, then!
  See! for I wear
Latest of bonnets,
  Last twist of hair;
French gloves and laces, —
  What more can I need?"
Laughed mighty Juno,
  "A lady, indeed!"

"I am a lady born!
  I have a name!
An unbroken ancestry
  Settles my claim."
"Weak!" said Minerva;
  "Irrelevant too!
Substitute ladyhood
  Never will do."

"I am a lady!
  No token of toil
Is on my fine fingers, —
  Vulgarity's soil!
I mix with no workfolk!"
  "Ah?" Venus exclaimed;
"*I* wedded a blacksmith,
  And was not ashamed.

"What face, bright as Hebe's,
  Illumines yon street?
That beautiful maiden
  Gives beggars their meat;
Her graceful hand leads them
  To honor and peace.
My sigh for lost ladies,"
  Said Venus, "I cease."

"I too!" called Minerva;
  And pointed to where
In a dreary log school-house,
  A girl, young and fair,
Spent life, strength, and beauty. —
  "She scatters live seed!
She works in wild thought-fields,
  The starved soul to feed."

Cried Juno, "Yon farm-wife,
  With white arms like mine,
Round, snowy loaves shaping,
  To me seems divine.
She, moulded a goddess,
  Who yet can prefer
To be useful and helpful, —
  What lady like her?"

Nodded the sky-women,
  Glad, one by one.
" Still there are ladies left
  Under the sun.

" Counterfeit creatures
  May borrow the name;
But the deep-seeing heavens
  Accept not their claim."

" Lady is loaf-giver!"
  Echoed the three.
" Who stays the world's hunger,
  True lady is she!"

"That suits me, Esther," Minta said. " You know
I am Minerva's lady half the year;
That is to say, I deal out learning's pap
To country babes, in District Number Three,
Under Chocorua's shadow. In plain words,
I am a schoolma'am in the summer-time,
As now I am a Lady of the Loom.
Come up and see me, girls! I'll give you bread
White as that Juno-woman's in the song,

Made with my own hands, too. And you may feast
Your eyes on stones,—our mountain-peaks,—besides;
All you down-country folks are fond of them."

"How beautiful!" said Esther. "If we could!"
For Esther, born of Puritans by the sea
That washes Plymouth Rock, within the curve
Of the long arm that Cape Cod reaches out
Toward Cape Ann's shoulder, never yet had seen
The mountains, save in glamour of her dreams.

"Come, then, for Eleanor's sake! Her cheeks will
bloom
With pinks in place of lilies. Quite too much
Of the fine-lady look her pale face wears
For any working-girl. With yellow cream,
Raspberries, brook-trout, and mountain-blackberries,
We'll make a woman of her," Minta said.

"'Lady' again!" cried Isabel. "Now I know
There's something more in it than feeding folks
With bread or with ideas. Eleanor says
I look a lady; you say she looks one.
I think it's in the dress, the air, the gait—"

"Yes, there 's a ladyish drawl and wriggle, too,
Easy enough to catch ; and furbelows—
Made usually of silk or satin, though,"
Said Minta, giving Isabel's gown a twitch
Upon its fluttering ruffles, which betrayed
Faint reminiscences of yesterday
Among the looms, in sundry spots of grease.
Strange! Eleanor, in her large coarse apron wrapped,
Walked past the oily wheels immaculate,
As saints have trodden on coals without a smirch;
While Isabel groaned daily over stains
Almost indelible.

With Isabel's face
After her reddening like an angry cloud,
Minta retreated ; vanishing from sight
In the room's farthest shadow.

Esther spoke,
Half to herself, half to the other two:
"Not long ago I read a doleful wail
From some town-dame, that now even factory-girls
Shine with gold watches, and you cannot tell,
Therefore, who are the ladies. Well-a-day!
If one could buy and hang about the neck

The ornament of a meek and quiet spirit,
'T would make a bawble even of that."

"But say,
Esther, whom do you call a lady?"

"She,
Dear Isabel, who is so in her mind, —
Harbors no millinery jealousies,
Holds no conventional standards. She may wear
Dainty kid gloves, or wear no gloves at all;
May work at wash-boards or embroidery-frames:
This is her mark, — she lives not for herself.
Our Lord has given us 'Service' for a badge.
True ladies, following him, seek not to be
Ministered unto, but to minister."

Then all grew thoughtful; whereat Eleanor,
With gentle tact, called out, —

"A hymn! a tune!
Let us sing, sisters, now the preaching's done!
Look! how the slanting sunbeams light the slope
Across the river!"

And her voice arose
Clear as an oriole's, in a grand psalm-tune
Married to one of Watts' old-fashioned hymns: —

"There everlasting spring abides,
And never-withering flowers.
Death, like a narrow sea, divides
This heavenly land from ours.

"Sweet fields beyond the swelling flood
Stand dressed in living green;
So to the Jews old Canaan stood,
While Jordan rolled between."

Then, as a spring becomes a rivulet,
The notes grew light; psalms bubbled into songs,
Songs into ballads, — homely Scottish strains
That vibrate on the heart-strings as no flight
Or fall of operatic somerset
Can ever. Eleanor's unschooled notes fled on
Through the swan-music of the "Land o' the Leal,"
"My ain Countree," and tender "Auld Lang Syne,"
Touched many an ancient border-melody,
And slipped through carol, roundelay, and catch
So liltingly, the others joined, perforce.

Meanwhile the river rose, and downward bore
Strange booty, stolen from the upper farms, —

A fence, a hen-coop, torn roots of old trees,
And once a little cottage, half unroofed.
That stopped the music, and the singers three
Leaned out in wonder, while their thoughts went up
To the stream's far-off sources.
                                        And they talked,
While the slow day slid into afternoon,
Of Minta's mountain-home; of summits gray
Rising from mist, or hiding in deep cloud;
Of the great land-slips; and the placid lakes,
Mirrors of haughty peaks; of the strong flood
Rushing below them, — how its infancy
Lay cradled amid blue Franconia hills,
Laughing up at the Old Man of the Notch,
Whose stony face into far Nothing looks
With all a mortal wise-head's gravity;
Of Conway intervales, their carpets green
Laid broad and soft before the vast rock-gate
Into the sanctuary of the hills;
And of dark passes to that cloud-crowned peak
Which bears the name the New World most reveres.
And Esther, longing, said, "What think you, girls?
Can we afford to go?"
                                Pale Eleanor
Looked up, her face moonlighted with a smile

Of pleasure at the thought; while Isabel
Grew serious, thinking of her empty purse,
On which her ribbons flamed a commentary;
But said, —
"O, I know mountains well enough!
Hard-faced old neighbors in the wilds of Maine,
Where I spent all my childhood. I will wait
Here for my fairy prince and godmother,
While you go browsing on the Granite Hills."

Just then the overseer, passing by them, said,
"A holiday! The river's will is up
To stop the mills, and for a while you are free."

It was a welcome word. The three glad girls
Slipped off work-aprons, bonnets caught, and shawls,
And went out for a walk among green trees,
Like souls released from earth to Paradise.

II.

BESIDE the river one girl walked alone,
While these sang from their window.
                                        Wistful, grave,
Beneath a firm, large forehead bloomed her eyes,
Two violets shadowed by a rock. A face
Not beautiful, nor plain, that in you left
A lingering wish to look on it again,
And speak to the spirit behind it.
                                        As she walked,
Her thoughts, in silence, talked among themselves : —

" My Merrimack, I am a homesick girl
To you I tell the secret, you alone.
I think but as a hireling of my work,
The work that looked like a romantic sport
Ere I began it. Woof of poetry
Through some coarse, homely warp forever runs !

Our farm-house 'mid the hills, — I see it now
Framed in the fine gold of Romance.

"Ah me!
How can I like the clatter of the looms,
The grime, the dust, the heat, the dizzy din,
The many faces!

"Hark! some girls are glad!
I hear their happy songs above me. Light,
And tinkling clear, as a harmonica,
The music trickles through the evening red
And ripples down the river. 'Bonnie Doon'
Dies on the air like an exhaling tear.
And hush again! 'Sweet Afton's' lullaby
Puts bird and leaf to sleep.

"You comfort me,
Bright faces blooming out into the sky;
Seen through the wind-swayed tassels of the birch,
You make me think of angels. And why not?
What of that dingy background? So they go
And come, across the moil and toil of earth;
And lend a hand to keep life's weaving smooth.
You and your work are but a little lower,
To One who hears, your song may be as sweet.
Out of that strange, confused machinery
You bring white raiment for the forms of men,
As angels may for souls.

"Fain, fain would I
Be happy in my toil, with you! But sad
I am, and loneliness awakens fear.
What unknown grief awaits me? Tell me, Fate!"

She sat down on a mossy stump, where now
The long, straight spears of sunset struck out gold
From emerald intense. A letter, sealed,
She held before her, studying the words
Upon its face, as if the hand that wrote
Were unfamiliar, yet well known. The seal
She broke at last, slowly, unwillingly,
But waited, sitting there as in a dream.

A girlish voice rang softly through the trees
Beside the vesper-sparrow's. Eleanor,
From her companions strayed a little way,
Sang a low hymn among the violets.

THEY neither toil nor spin;
  And yet their robes have won
A splendor never seen within
  The courts of Solomon.

Tints that the cloud-rifts hold,
  And rainbow-gossamer,
The violet's tender form enfold;
  No queen is draped like her.

All heaven and earth and sea
  Have wrought with subtlest power
That clothed in purple she might be, —
  This little fading flower.

We, who must toil and spin,
  What clothing shall we wear?
The glorious raiment we shall win
  Life shapes us everywhere.

God's inner heaven hath sun,
  And rain, and space of sky,
Wherethrough for us his spindles run,
  His mighty shuttles fly.

His seamless vesture white
  He wraps our spirits in;
He weaves his finest webs of light
  For us, who toil and spin.

The silent girl, lost in her letter's fold,
Heard hymn and bird-song as she heard the wind,
Listening to none of them. Something she read
Hurt her, as by a sudden, secret blow.
It seemed to her as if a mist had fallen
Among the trees; the pallid river ran
Receding in gray distance. "Is it death?"
She murmured. "If it be death, it is well."
And sank in cold unconsciousness.

A step
Was on the turf beside her. Eleanor,
Stooping to pluck a pale anemone, saw
A paper fall, a hand as colorless
Drop with it; heard a woman's moan, and ran,
Fluttered and awed, to lift the brow that lay,
Whiter than marble, among flickering leaves.
Esther and Isabel, farther down the bank,
Returned at Eleanor's call. Before they came,
The stranger's eyes half opened, closed again,
Then opened wide, and looked around amazed.
"Lean on me," Eleanor said; "you must be ill."
"Ill? All is ill. I thought — I thought I died;
I thought I saw an angel, coming through
The gates of pearl. The trees of heaven were green;
A river ran by. Alas! it is the earth, —

A world I cannot live in." "We are friends,"
Said Eleanor. "Trust us, dear." And as she spoke,
With stealthy haste the open letter slipped
Into the stranger's bosom, doubting not
It held some bitter secret.

She, revived,
Under the ministerings of the three,
Arose, and, moaning thanks, would fain have gone,
And left them there. But Esther, quietly
Putting an arm about her, led her up
In tender silence to the homeward road.
The other two went slowly by themselves,
Not seeing Esther more till evening fell.
Then, in their room,—scant lodging had these three
Among a weary house-full, twenty girls,
Who ate and slept beneath one roof,—where they
One small apartment shared, and called it home,—
In their own room together, Esther told
The stranger's name, Ruth Woodburn; and she said
Her friendship would be gain to them: her words,
Her every tone, showed culture. And besides,
She seemed as one by trouble stupefied,—
Was all alone in a strange house, with girls
Of the ill-bred, hoydenish sort, and others, too,
Of the small, peeping species, who delight

To pick and pry at sorrow's keyless lock.
"She is next door to Minta Summerfield,
But Minta has not met her, and I doubt
If Minta's mirth would be good medicine
For one like her. If I had but a home
To give her mothering in!"
"But, Esther, dear,
To us your heart is mother, shelter, home;
Let her, too, find it so," said Eleanor.
"Will she not come to us?"
And still the friends
Murmured for the sad stranger gentle plans,
Until the lights were out, and through their thoughts
The stillness of the house stole in, with sleep.

III

NEXT morning's sun rose on a silent town.
The swollen river noiselessly moved past
The quiet mills, — less river now than lake.
In the red dawn the drowsy girls awoke
To the bell's usual clang, that summoned them
From dreams to labor. At the stroke of five
All laggards saw the gates against them swing.
To-day, however, the great working-crowd
Surged in and out awhile; free passage left
For those who stayed to rub the steel-work bright,
Or clean the dangerous wheels while they stood still.

Esther, alone, sought Ruth; and on the way
Met Minta Summerfield, who seemed disturbed
And strangely sobered.

"Esther, some one 's sick
In the next house. I overheard the girls
Talking about her; saying that she mopes,

And will not eat, nor tell them how she ails;
That when she speaks, 't is all in grand book-talk,
Learned as college-folks; they hinted, too,
That she was some fine lady in disgrace,
Come here to hide from sight.

"O, girls can be
So cruel to one another! I am vexed
That I am one, sometimes! Do, Esther, do
Go and look after her, or I shall rush
At those girls like a whirlwind."

Esther smiled;
With a brief whisper smoothed out Minta's frown,
And disappeared.

Poor Ruth! There was no need
Of many words. To Esther's pleasant voice,
She yielded, like a child, and let herself
Be dressed, and led to Esther's room, and laid
On Esther's bed, who sat beside her there,
With kind pretence of book and sewing-work,
Her two companions taking holiday
In a long ramble up the river-side.

Ruth lightly dozed. Esther, intent to keep
The slumberer undisturbed, let drop her work,
And yielded herself partly to her book

(Poems of Wordsworth, Eleanor's New-Year's gift),
And partly to the south-wind's tenderness,
While memory led her back beside the sea,
Where she had played with many little ones
In childhood, on a sunny homestead-slope,
The deep, eternal murmur of the waves
Upbearing on its monotone the song
Of bluebird, wren, and robin, blending all
In a wild, sweet entanglement. Home-dreams,
As in all womanly souls, made undertone
To her life's music. But her hopes and plans
And fancies were a garden builded in
Behind great walls of duty. Her true work
She sought the clew of, here 'mid endless threads
Shaped from crude cotton into useful cloth.

Not always to be here among the looms, —
Scarcely a girl she knew expected that;
Means to one end their labor was, — to put
Gold nest-eggs in the bank, or to redeem
A mortgaged homestead, or to pay the way
Through classic years at some academy;
More commonly to lay a dowry by
For future housekeeping.

But Esther's thought

Was none of these; unshaped and vague it lay, —
A hope to spend herself for worthy ends.
Aliens were in her childhood's home. No past
Could be revived for her, and all her heart
Went forth into the Future's harvest-field,
A Ruth who never of a Boaz dreamed.
Whatever work came, whoso crossed her path,
Lonely as this pale stranger, wheresoe'er
She saw herself a need, there should be home,
Business, and family. She raised her eyes,
As her soul said Amen to this resolve,
And saw Ruth languidly peruse her face
Through mists of thought; who murmured, "Read
aloud."

A smile from Esther answered. She began
Where her eyes fell. Laodamia's tale
It chanced to be, with its heroic thoughts
Climbing sharp crags of sorrow to high faith.
Ruth listened, musing, till she heard the words,
"Learn by a mortal yearning to ascend,
Seeking a higher object." Then she sobbed.
"It is too hard, too hard! Read something else;
A song, a ballad, anything!"
"Dear child,

The time will come for this too," Esther said ;
" But now your nerves are strained, and you are ill ;
Of that I was too thoughtless."
And she took
Another volume from the hanging shelf,
The three girls' library.
The one she chose
Was a strange medley-book of prose and rhyme
Cut from odd magazines, or pages dim
Of yellow journals, long since out of print ;
And pasted in against the faded ink
Of an old log-book, relic of the sea,
And mostly filled with legends of the shore
That Esther loved, her home-shore of Cape Ann.
" Here is a doggerel tale of witchcraft-time
Some one has reeled off since they laid the rails
From Boston eastward. Ruth, you need not try
To hear it ; let it croon you off to sleep."

PEGGY BLIGH'S VOYAGE.

You may ride in an hour or two, if you will,
From Halibut Point to Beacon Hill,
With the sea beside you all the way,
Through pleasant places that skirt the Bay ;

By Gloucester Harbor and Beverly Beach,
Salem's old steeples, Nahant's long reach,
Blue-bordered Swampscott, and Chelsea's wide
Marshes, laid bare to the drenching tide,
With a glimpse of Saugus spire in the west,
And Malden hills in their dreamy rest.

All this you watch idly, and more by far,
From the cushioned seat of a railway-car.
But in days of witchcraft it was not so;
City-bound travellers had to go
Horseback over a blind, rough road,
Or as part of a jolting wagon-load
Of garden produce and household goods,
Crossing the fords, half lost in the woods,
By the fear of redskins haunted all day,
And the roar of lions, some histories say.

If ever for Boston a craft set sail,
Few to secure a passage would fail,
Who had errands to do in the three-hilled town:
And they *might* return ere the sun went down.
So, one breezy midsummer dawn,
Skipper Nash, of the schooner Fawn,

Sails away with a crowded deck.
One of his passengers cranes her neck
Out of her scarlet cloak, — an eye
Like a smouldering coal had Peggy Bligh,—
And looks at her townsmen, looks at the sea,
At the crew and the skipper ; what can it be
That hinders their flinging her bold glance back ?
Many a wife hath an eye as black,
And a cloak as scarlet. Ay, but she —
Nobody covets her company !
Nobody meets that strange look of hers
But a nameless terror within him stirs,
His heart-strings flutter, his nerves they twitch, —
'T is an evil eye, — it will blight and bewitch.

Afraid to be silent, afraid to speak,
The crew and the skipper, with half-oaths weak,
Looked up dismayed when aboard she came,
And the voyagers whispered around her name,
And gazed askance, as apart she stood,
Eying them under her scarlet hood.

A fair wind wafted them down the Bay ;
By noon at the Boston wharves they lay.

"We shall sail at three!" the skipper cried;
Save Peggy, all were aware that he lied,
For along the deck had been passed a word
Which only speaker and listener heard, —
How he meant to give the old crone the slip
By an hour or so, on the homeward trip.

Errands all finished, and anchor weighed,
Out of the harbor her way she made, —
The schooner Fawn. But who hastens down
To the water-side, with a shout and frown,
Angrily stamps with her high-heeled shoe,
Audibly curses the skipper and crew,
Flutters her cloak and flames with her eye? —
Who but the witch-woman, old Peg Bligh?

"We 'll give her the go-by!" says Skipper Nash,
And laughs at his schooner's scurry and dash;
But here and there one muttered, "He 's rash!"
"As good right has Peggy," said one or two,
"To a homeward passage as I or you;
For what has the poor old beldam done
That any man could lay finger on,
Worse than living alone in a tumble-down hut,
And speaking her mind when she chose to? But —"

The speaker stopped, to follow the stare
Of his listeners up through the windy air.
A monstrous gull bore down on the blast;
Once it poised on the schooner's mast;
Once it flapped in the skipper's face;
Scarcely it veered for a moment's space
From the prow's white track in the seething brine;
Its sharp eye gleamed with a steel-cold shine,
And one of the sailors averred that he saw
A red strip dangle from beak and claw;
And all the voyagers shrank with fear
To see that wild creature a-swoop so near.

As they hove in sight of Salem town
A fog came up, and the breeze went down.
They could almost hear the farm-folk speak,
And smell the magnolias at Jeffrey's Creek.
Abreast of the Half-way Rock once more,
With the Misery Islands just off shore,
The gull gave a shriek, and flew out of sight,
And — there they lay in the fog all night.

They dared not stir until morn was red,
And the sky showed a blue streak overhead;
Then glad on the clear wave sped the Fawn

Homeward again through a breezy dawn,
And the skipper shouted, "The vessel arrives
In season for breakfast with your wives!"

But some one else had arrived before.
Who is that, by the hut on the shore,
Milking her cow with indifferent mien,
As if no schooner were yet to be seen!
By the side glance out of her small black eye,
It must be — surely it is — Peg Bligh!

How she got there no mortal could tell,
But crew and passengers knew right well
That she had not set foot upon deck or hull,
"Nor the mast?" About that you may ask the gull.

Well, the story goes on to say
That Skipper Nash always rued the day
When he left old Peg on the wharf behind,
With her shrill cry drifting along the wind.
For he lost his schooner, his children died,
And his wife; and his cattle and sheep beside;
And his old age found him alone, forlorn,
Wishing, no doubt, he had never been born.

What Peggy Bligh had to do with his case
It is hard to see, in our time and place.
How things might have struck us, we do not know,
Had we lived here two hundred years ago,
When the thoughts of men took a weirder shape
Than any mist that hangs round the Cape.
But this moral 's a good one for all to mind:
His own heart is the curse of a man unkind.

Ruth listened drowsily, as she was bid;
In gentle, wave-like trance she sank and rose,
Gazing on wall and ceiling, as if there
But by a dream's permission.
For the room
Showed legibly its inmates' daily life.
Isabel's couch, a sofa-bedstead, worn
And faded, stood against the whitewashed wall,
The birds-of-paradise upon its chintz
Dim-plumaged; and — perhaps by accident —
A red shawl, flung across the sofa's arm,
Concealed its shabbiness. Above it hung
A colored wood-cut, of an arch-faced girl
Crossing a brook, barefooted, with a smirk
Of half-coquettish fear. Near Esther's bed
Raphael's Madonna from an oval gazed,

The Virgin with her Child alone, engraved
In some old German town, a relic left
From Eleanor's home. The bookshelf swung between
Two simple prints, — the "Cotter's Saturday Night"
And the "Last Supper," dear to Esther's heart,
Though scarce true to Da Vinci. On the shelves
Maria Edgeworth's "Helen" leaned against
Thomas à Kempis. Bunyan's "Holy War"
And "Pilgrim's Progress" stood up stiff between
"Locke on the Understanding" and the Songs
Of Robert Burns. The "Voices of the Night,"
"Bridal of Pennacook," "Paradise Lost,"
With Irving's "Sketch-Book," "Ivanhoe," Watts's
Hymns,
Mingled in democratic neighborhood.
Upon a small, white-napkined table lay
Three Bibles, by themselves, — one almost new,
The others showing usage. Little need
To say the unworn one was Isabel's,
Who boasted it her only property
That was not worse for wear.
Ruth roused her thoughts
As Esther ceased, saying, —
"Poor old Peggy Bligh!
Is it a woman's fault not to be young?

To be left lonely? Men have held it so.
They blame us for misfortunes more than sins,
In their half-civilized instinct.

"But the sea!
Would I could rest myself on its unrest,
Drown in its vast complaint my little moan!
I never saw the sea."

"Nor mountains I,"
Said Esther; "tell me of them."

"Of myself
I 'll tell you first; it is your due to know
Something about me. Widowed now of him
Whose love of books I have inherited,
My mother keeps his farm at Holderness;
Dear village, in whose ancient church I learned
The Creed and Ten Commandments!

"Boys and books
Our house is full of; little else indeed.
One baby sister blossoms like a rose
Among her thorny brothers, all grown rough
With farm-work, and yet all with scholar-tastes.
Rich relatives I have. More doors than one
Would open to me, if I would but be
Adopted lady-daughter; but I choose
A way more independent, and am here."

Then, silent for a moment, she sighed out,
"O, life is hard and cold! and God himself
Is hid in heaven. And I — why was I born?"

Then Esther softly asked, "Is not God near
In every kind thought of a human heart?
Look on your pillow, Ruth!"

Turning her head,
With eyes tear-softened, the pale girl beheld
A knot of delicate flowers, — anemones,
Woven of wind and snow, and faintly flushed
As a babe's cheek; and violets blue, that breathed
A sweetness not of earth; and pale gold bells
Of uvularia; and a tuft or two
Of downy-stemmed rock-saxifrage, that brings
New England sea-crags their first hint of May;
And liverleaf, its satin-folded cups
Transparent, tinged with amethyst and rose.
All faintly colored, as our spring flowers are,
With fine, cool, elemental tints, — the light
Of pink and amber sunsets upon snow.

"How lovely! Were they dropped from heaven?"
asked Ruth;
For in her spasm of grief she heard no sound

Of Eleanor's light footfall, fading out
Soft as it entered. 'T was as if a breeze
Brought in the blossoms.
"I am sure God writes
In earthly hieroglyphics," Esther said,
"Some of his plainest gospels. Love alone,
Pure love, could paint in colors such as these.
Believe it! He cares more for your soul's health
Than any plant's."
Ruth's whispered prayer rose: "Thou
Who lovest thy children, if a drop of dew,
A sunbeam yet can reach me, bid me live!"

Then Esther kissed her brow. She, lying there,
Gazed on the flowers as if they talked with her.
Esther spoke not, for Heaven was in the room,
And through the fragrant silence seemed to glide
Light footsteps of invisible comforters.

IV.

Lightly across the fields tripped Isabel,
With Eleanor close beside her. To the rocks
They bent their footsteps, where Pawtucket Falls
Broke in upon the river's quietness
A mile or so, brawling between wide banks
Crimson with columbines far on through May,
And blue with nodding harebells until frost.
There grew the painted cup, a living coal
Upon the velvet sward; and there were mats
Of trailing twin-flower, sweet with memories
Of Swedish Linnæus; and a nameless wealth
Of wild bloom tangled in with forest-green.
Free rushed the rapid waters then, as free
As in the days when Passaconaway
Came hither with his warrior Pennacooks,
Encamping in the bending birch-tree's shade;
Free as when gentle Wannalancet came,

Trusting the Christians who betrayed him, till,
His hunting-grounds all gone, his tribe despoiled
And scattered, he turned northward his sad face,
Sped up the river with his remnant chiefs,
And hid himself behind the great White Hills.

Trim promenades and even rows of trees
Then were not, but around were broken crags,
With hemlocks leaning over, and green shelves
And mossy nooks where children came to play.
And here they found a group of little girls
Watching the course of the mad stream.
Said one,
"I walked across to Dracut Side last year,
Just where it runs the swiftest now."
And one, —
"I wish the freshet would keep on a week,
And then we need not work, but every day
Could play here by the river."
"Do you work,
You little girls?"
"O yes, indeed we do!
We change the bobbins in the spinning-room.
Our mothers need the money that we earn.
Three months we go to school; the rest we work."
"How old are you?" asked Eleanor.

"Thirteen.
Ann is eleven. She is taller, though,
Than I am; stronger, mother says. Those girls —
I do not know their ages. Ann and I, —
Alice — are sisters. Those are neighbors' girls."

"It is a pity!" Eleanor thought aloud.
"Are you not very tired sometimes?"
"O yes!
But so is everybody. We must learn,
While we are children, how to do hard things,
And that will toughen us, so mother says;
And she has worked hard always. When I first
Learned to doff bobbins, I just thought it play.
But when you do the same thing twenty times, —
A hundred times a day, — it is so dull!"

"But then," spoke up the bashful Ann, "you know
It is so nice between whiles, playing games,
And guessing riddles in the window-seats.
Sometimes the spinners are such pleasant girls, —
They come and play with us. But some are cross,
And some say dreadful words; if mother knew,
She would not let us work there. But we must,
And so we do not tell her."

While they talked,
Eleanor's mind went wandering opposite ways ;
Through the strange story of a little child
Earning its living, and to Esther's side,
Soothing a troubled soul.
"Dear Isabel,
If Esther could but see and smell the woods !
Handling these flowers, I touch the robes of May
Now close upon us. Stay here, while I run
Home with them to her."
Later, a half-hour,
Returning by the winding river-road,
A curve abrupt surprised her face to face
With two men, one her minister and friend,
A Christian gentleman, who cared for all
His brethren of God's family, nor asked
What creed they held, though strict his own.
The grace
To hold a firm opinion, yet unite
With men of differences as fixed, he had.
He knew that souls more truly meet in love
Than doctrine ; that to work in fellowship
Only with those whose thoughts link in with ours,
Is to put chain-gangs before angel-bands.
Like Chaucer's Parson, well he loved his books,

But better still Christ's lore, and Christ's dear flock.
And he had chosen to watch these scattered lambs
Gathered from all New England's pasturage
Rather than tend an easier fold, and live
With his compeers in taste and learning. Him
Eleanor greeted, with a happy light
Of recognitionin her grateful eyes.

They went their separate ways. The pastor's friend
Asked, musingly, "Where have I seen that face?"

"In vision, possibly; well worthy she
To inspire a young man's dream, to haunt him with
Life's noblest possibilities."
"But no!
Somewhere on earth those eyes and mine have met;
She is too pale for health, though."
"Now you speak
Professionally, Doctor, as you should,
A thoroughbred physician. Eleanor Gray —"

"Gray? Gray? If she were from Connecticut
She might be — my third cousin."
"May be, — is.
That is her native State."
"Permit me, sir,

To call upon her with you ; each must know
The other's kindred, if we are not kin."

"You understand my guardianship, good friend,
Of such young women ?—for at present she
Is of my parish."
"Such young women, sir ?
A face like that stands guardian for itself.
Moreover, the reserve of thoughtfulness
And culture stamp it visibly. The best
Home-influences must be hers."
"Have been, no doubt,
But she is orphaned, and a factory-girl."

The young man started.
"How ? it cannot be!"
Not strange was his surprise, first visiting
To-day the youthful City of Work ; for rare
In any town are countenances pure
And fair as Eleanor's ; and all he knew
Of factory working-girls had reached him through
Traditions of Old England.
"Are there, sir,
Many like her here ? Such a menial life
Poorly befits her bearing. I should blush

To see my sister drudging in these mills
As in a prison-shop. More delicate
This young girl looks than any sister of mine."

Good Pastor Alwyn smiled.
"Not many such
As Eleanor Gray, perhaps, this side of heaven,
Where she will be called early. You ascribe
Strange magic to our spindles, let me say,
Fancying their touch an injury to her
Who tends them. Character is not the stuff
That circumstance can spoil, — my gospel reads.
And, if it were, inside those factory walls
The daughters of our honest yeomanry,
Children of tradesmen, teachers, clergymen,
Their own condition make in mingling. True,
The scum and dross are here, as everywhere,
When human elements mix; but like seeks like
In all societies, and therefore here:
New England women are what these girls are.
— Yes, you shall call with me on Eleanor Gray
And Esther Hale, and own yourself unjust."
Eleanor, meanwhile, again had reached the Falls,
Between whose rifts of sound a merry swell
Of children's voices floated on the wind: —

WILL the fairy-folk come back,
  Such as haunt old stories,
Sliding down the moonbeam's track,
  Hid in morning-glories?
Air is warp, and sun is weft;
Is a rainbow spinner left?

No; not one. They never will!
  Streams they loved are busy
Turning spindles in the mill;
  Turning mill-folk dizzy.
Toil is warp, and money weft;
Not a fairy loom is left.

Noise has frightened them away
  From their greenwood places;
Never would they spend a day
  Among careworn faces.
Gather up the warp and weft:
See if anything is left!

Merry days go dancing by;
  Hard work comes, and tarries.
Why, for that, wind sigh through sigh?
  Children, we 'll be fairies!

Life is warp, and love is weft;
Children's hearts and hands are left.

After the song a pretty picture! High
Upon a swarded crag, a mimic throne
Under a canopy of evergreen;
And, shrinking back into a heap of flowers,
The timid Ann! the goldenest of crowns
The meadows could afford, upon her head.
Her playmates all as waiting-maids adorned
With coronals of sapphire, opal, pearl,
As each had chosen her blossom's tint; with lengths
Of trailing ground-pine passed from hand to hand
In a green network, weaving in and out
Fantastic dance and chant: their downcast queen
Flushed and abashed, her dimples curved with shame,
And restive under dignities unsought.
They called to Eleanor: "See, it is Queen Ann!
We chained her up and put her on a throne.
She wants to wander off and gather flowers;
But we are stronger: she must be our queen!"

And then they played around her the old games
Of Queen Anne sitting in the sun, to read
Her royal lover's letters; of King George

And the two armies, marshalling to the tune
Of "Oranges!" or "Lemons!" and quaint sports
Brought in the May-Flower out of Mother-Land.
Amid the frolic Isabel threw herself
Into the children's ring.
"Look! look! a dog!"
Cried Alice, pointing to mid-stream. "O dear!
He s drowning! no! now, see! he swims this way!
Good dog! come here!"
The child unheedfully
Reached forward, slipped. Black eddies swirled beneath.
But Isabel caught her as she slid, and both
Seemed for an instant doomed. A moment more,
And both were safe. Then the dog leaped ashore,
Whining towards Isabel.
The games broke up;
The children led scared Alice home, and Ann
Went sobbing, under her forgotten crown.
Eleanor drew Isabel among the trees,
Nerveless, herself, and trembling. Her gay friend
Had wrenched her wrist, but that was all, she said,
Smiling at her mishap.
"You risked your life!"
Cried Eleanor.

"Which was not a serious risk!
Not much of a life: I think I 'd sell it cheap.
What 's in your basket, Eleanor? I 'm faint
With hunger, and you look as pale as death."

They ate their simple lunch. The shaggy dog
Lingered, and shared it with them. Slowly then
They sauntered onward, over the long bridge,
Where first the river makes its downward plunge,
And spent some hours among the Dracut pines.

Crossing again, near dusk, they passed a group;
Ladies, and a young man, with cloak and cane
Carried right gracefully. As Isabel turned
He colored, so did she. The dog rushed up
From some erratic search beneath the bridge,
Following his master with a joyful bark.

Eleanor's eyes asked plainly, "Who?" No word
Spoke Isabel, till they came in sight again
Of the red boarding-houses; then she said,
"Don't mention this to Esther!" nothing more;
And Eleanor, in her shocked surprise, was dumb.

A stir was in the street. Not many doors
From theirs, a group of men set down a bier

Whereon a drowned girl lay, whom they had found
Above the locks, within a lonesome bend
Of the canal.
"What? did she drown herself?"
"Was no one with her?" "Had she any friends?"
Questioned the standers-by. A whisper, then,
Started by some one, ran from mouth to mouth :
"She was alone here. In her early days
One slip she made, — you see she is not young;
For that she never could forgive herself,
And she has toiled in silence ever since,
Upright and honest, but too sad to care
For friends or life. If death were accident
Or purpose, none can tell."
"O, pitiful!"
Cried Eleanor's heart, as on, with covered eyes,
She drew the fascinated Isabel,
Whose gaze was fixed upon the dripping hair
And half-closed eyelids.
"O, too pitiful!
Why did not Esther know her? Was there none
To tell her she might put her weight of sin
Behind her, and walk on with other girls
In peaceful pathways, happy and forgiven?
Would we had helped her!"

Slowly Isabel moved,
Still looking backward at those glassy eyes,
Speaking no word until the house-door shut
Behind them, then upon the stairway sank,
And sobbed, as if she saw in that girl's fate
Some dreadful possibility of her own.

V.

SABBATH upon the river and the hills!
And Sabbath-rest among the weary wheels,
That ceased their groaning with a conscious hush.
Sabbath to lives unwound from labor's coil;
One welcome pause between dull sentences
Of week-long prose.
                                        That Sabbath in the air
Which made New England as old Palestine, —
An Olivet of every green ascent,
With Kedron or Siloam flowing past,
In windings of familiar streams, — how vast
Its depth and height of stillness! Every leaf
Of every tree seemed whispering reverently
Sóme Hebrew tale or parable. The sky
Came close to earth, as bending to let down
The glory of the New Jerusalem.
That sweet, old-fashioned day has left us now,
With inspirations and with presences

Which never can return. It is a part
Of our lost Puritan inheritance.
Whatever better this new time has brought,
Never again the land shall know that rest,
That inexpressible calm.

Together walked,
Under May's fragrant sunshine, Eleanor Gray
And Esther Hale, amid the churchward crowd
That filled brick-paven streets and sandy roads
With pleasant color. Maidens robed in white,
With gypsy-hats blue-ribboned; maidens gay
In silk attire; and maidens Quaker-prim,
With gingham gowns, straw bonnets, and smooth hair, —
Girl Baptists, Universalists, Methodists,
Girl Unitarians and Orthodox, —
Sought each their separate temple, while a few
Entered the green enclosure of Saint Ann's,
Still left, an oasis of vine-wreathed stones,
Amid the city's dust.

Here, close on Ruth,
Isabel followed, all in rosy haste,
Saying, "Let me go with you to-day; I like
Your church, Ruth Woodburn," — though it was her wont

To sit with Eleanor in the singing-seats
Where Pastor Alwyn preached; a steeple-house,
Barn-like, brick-red, and angular, and yet
To those who worshipped there, a gate of heaven.
For the good pastor's most unworldly soul,
While all alive to solemn harmonies
Of heavenly truth, quivered through every chord
With sympathy intense: a tenderness
As of some grief divine was in his voice,
Picturing man's loss through sin; but when his theme
Was sin's immortal Conqueror, the Lord
Of Love, the Life and Light of men,
It was as if the Master had himself
Entered in, with his beautiful "All Hail!"
And "I am with you alway." So the house
Was like some common face irradiate
With inward nobleness, fairer than fair.

And Pastor Alwyn's manly lineaments
To-day caught radiance from his text, the words
"As seeing Him who is invisible."

The sermon was as fresh as springtide air
Whispering through trees in bloom outside. He held
His Bible as a living book, not dry,

Dead leaves of Judæan growth, whose preciousness
Was in their sacred legendary scent,
But a perennial plant, acclimated
Wherever any flower of heaven can breathe.
And words like these he spoke, remembered well
By more than two girls into after-years.

"As seeing Thee! And must we turn from earth
To find Thee, Lord? 'No,' Thou dost answer us
From Cana, where thy touch of miracle
Made marriage-mirth flow free with the new wine.
'No,' from the inn-seat, where thou joinedst in talk
With loitering fisherman and publican.
'No,' from the market-place, where children danced
And piped amid their elders' wearier game
Of usury and barter. Thou didst blame,
More than all other sin, the Pharisee's,
Shutting his sanctimonious eyelids close
In on himself, a whited sepulchre
Opaque, that hid from sight the present God,
Made manifest by little children's lips,
And bird-songs, and the speechless lily's breath.

"Dear Lord, the nearer we approach to Thee,
We find that thou wert with us all the while

In common things; for every innocent sport,
The blameless thought that bubbles in a laugh,
No less than visions awful and sublime,
Thine image and thy superscription wear.
How shall we ever know thee, knowing not
Thou dwellest with us in clay tabernacles,
And beckonest upward through beseeching eyes
Of men who struggle and aspire toward thee?

"'Blessed are the pure in heart; they shall see God.'
And as thou clearest our soul's sight, we behold
The Infinite where we little thought him hid.
The clod a diamond flashes. Our dim earth
Holds the sun's elements, and by a touch
Like that which swung it forth in space, might be
Transmuted into pure, impalpable light.
Empty of thee is nothing thou hast made.

"This, Lord, is life: to know thee in thy gifts,
And in thy messengers; to recognize
In all things visible, thee, the Invisible God,
The Soul that lives in human souls, the Friend
Whose hint and shadow earthly friendship is.

" And have we dreamed the Christ of God could die
When the man Jesus passed from sight? He lives,
Eternal as the Father. Through all years
The Love which is both human and divine
Stoops to our scarred, sick race, to lift it up
Unto the stature of the Perfect Man.
His breath is in us, as the breath of May
Is in the happy flowers. Sin is sole death.
If our life bloom, it is because He lives
Who is the Resurrection and the Life."

Then, with a prayer which gathered into one
All hearts, and laid them on the Eternal Heart;
With the doxology, all voices blent
In grand " Old Hundred's " firm uplift of praise;
The benediction, " Peace be with you all,
Now and forever," — forth into the air,
Sweet as Eve's garden breathed, the people passed.

And is there any climate, any land,
More beautiful than our New England is,
This blossom-week of May, when east-winds pause,
Relenting, dying down to whispers light
As Zephyr's own, along the rosy leagues
Of orchard-skirting roads, through village lanes

And over cottage gardens? Can the air
Have wandered with as delicate a breath
Through famed Hesperides? In rose-lined flakes
The apple-petals dropped, as Eleanor Gray
And Esther lengthened out their homeward walk, —
A perfumed snow-fall; and from Eleanor's lips
There fell a gentle, rhythmic murmuring: —

Apple-blossoms, budding, blowing,
In the soft May air:
Cups with sunshine overflowing, —
Flakes of fragrance, — drifting, snowing,
Showering everywhere!

Fairy promises, outgushing
From the happy trees!
White souls into love-light blushing, —
Love and joy to utterance rushing, —
Are ye not like these?

Such an overflow of sweetness
Needs the heart of spring;
In her wealth of bloom is meetness,
Though to the ripe fruit's completeness
All she may not bring.

Words are more than idle seeming, —
  Blossoms of good-will.
What she would do, Love is dreaming;
What she can, ashamed of scheming,
  Cramped and stinted still.

Apple-blossoms, billowy brightness
  On the tide of May,
O, to wear your rose-touched whiteness!
Flushing into bloom, with lightness
  To give life away!

"Isabel, Isabel! Oh, where have you been?
The sermon was like poetry."
                    "Poh! child!"
I 'm glad I did not hear it, then; I like
Plain prose much better! Truth is, Eleanor,
I 'm sick of Sunday doings." And she threw
Gay scarf and veil and parasol aside,
And yawned: "You know I am a heathen, dear,
And good folks bore me. Esther now, and you,
I can endure; I know your weaknesses;
You are not saints yet, will not be, while I
Am here to thorn you!"

"Now, dear Isabel,
What has gone wrong?"

"Ah, well! not anything
Except myself, a 'wretched child of wrath,'
So Sister Sterne says. She has called me names
All the way home; she must 'take up her cross,'
She told me, — and she made me cross enough!
I 'd rather be a Patagonian
Than such a Christian!"

"Well, but at Saint Ann's
Nobody vexed you?"

"No; the ups and downs
Just suit my restlessness. The prayer-book place, —
That bothers me, though!"

"Ah, now, Isabel,
Who was the gentleman that handed you
His velvet prayer-book over the pew back?
I thought he knew you —"

Ruth looked up dismayed
At Isabel's gesture.

"Why should you think that?
Any one finds the place, and hands the book,
In your church, Ruth."

Then, seeing Eleanor
Gaze at her with sad wonder, turned at bay,

And asked, "Hem! Eleanor, was young Doctor Mann
In the pastor's pew to-day? And did he look
Impressed as usual, at you in the choir?
If he called on you once when you were out,
I think he 'll call again; don't you?"
They laughed, —
All the girls now; for Esther had come in
With Minta Summerfield, and to fling hints
At Eleanor about sweethearts, seemed absurd
As striking matches in a lily's cup.

With the new-comers the talk changed, for this
Was Esther's hour, the after-service hour,
When each spoke her free word, her deepest thought
Or lightest doubt, and Esther, as she could,
Suggested answer.
O, what questionings
Of fate and freedom, of how evil came,
And what death is, and what the life to come,
Passed to and fro among these girls! For all
But Ruth and Minta were from childhood bred
On the tough meat of Calvin's doctrines; food
For logical digestion, given to babes
By Pilgrim nursing-fathers.
Now their speech

Was of a lecture heard the bygone week
By Esther and by Minta; a grand theme, —
"Law," — and its treatment philosophical,
By a great thinker. When he boldly said,
"What use in prayer? No beggar shall change Law, —
Law, which is God himself made known to man.
What use in prayer? Are not the laws of God,
Even as His nature is, unalterable?"
The two girls exchanged glances with amaze;
And Minta said, at closing, "Esther Hale,
Tell us, next Sunday, what you think of this."
So now again she spoke: "Esther, you know
I am a Methodist, and praying is
Two thirds of our religion; yet I felt
Stirred strangely, half convinced by that man's words.
Our preacher spoke of them to-day; declared
Philosophy is of the Devil; but that —
My own sect I may judge — is ignorance."

"Your sect!" said Isabel, breaking in, with heat.
"I wish it were a little more polite,
Less noisy, too. What right has Sister Sterne
To quiz me all about my 'state of mind,'
Ask if I read my Bible, if I pray,
If I am fit for heaven? — no! not for hers,

Nor would be, if I could! The other day
She held a meeting, when the looms were still,
Just before bell-time, in the window-seat.
O, how they sung and shouted! I cried out, —
I had a dreadful headache, — 'Do, do be
A little quieter!' Then Sister Sterne
Groaned, 'Isabel! if you ever get to heaven,
You'll have to hear a much worse noise than this!'"

"Now, now!" cried Eleanor, "such a Methodist
Is no fair specimen. Does Minta stun
Us with her shouts? And Pastor Alwyn says
He thanks God for John Wesley, and would like
To cry 'Amen!' to every earnest prayer."

"Enough!" laughed Minta. "Now I'll hold my tongue
About the stiff-necked, straight-laced Orthodox, —
My dearest friends, for all that! But I wish —
Esther, what paper is that in your hand?
I've seen you scribbling something all the week
On torn leaves, wrappings, — here, there, everywhere!
Is it not something for us?"

"Yes, it is.
That lecture sent me back through all the years
That I have lived. I know I have believed

God listens for our thoughts, and answers us;
But how much asking is sincere, and what
The real prayer is, and what it seeks and finds,
I have been querying. Now shall I read
What I have written?"

Then even Isabel
Settled herself against the sofa's arm
In listening posture; and the other girls
Cried eagerly, "Do!" and this is what she read:—

It was a meeting-going world wherein
My childhood found itself. The Sabbath sun
Warmed palsied footsteps up the windy slope,
Where rosy weanlings toddled breathlessly
In prints of patriarchal feet. It shone
Through lattice-work of apple-boughs in spring
Stained with pink glory of bloom, on silver hair
And flaxen baby-ringlets, on the heads
Of youngsters awkward with strange consciousness
Of smoothness, and on brows demure
Of arch girls Sunday-prim.

The sun himself
Lost in the pews the look of every day,—
His frolic look,—was cool, sedate, and blank.

In the tall pulpit rose the minister,
And talked of dispensations and decrees,
Of covenants, purposes, and ordinances,
Saints' perseverance, the church-militant,
Till to my vague child-thought the way to heaven
Seemed somehow built of sounding sentences
That went up through the roof, and shaped themselves
Like rafters, beams, and rafters, endlessly.
Alas! I knew I should lose footing there!
The men and women, with grown minds, could climb;
But I, poor fledgling, fallen on the pew-floor
Helpless and weak, the sky so very far,
And all that Babel-staging raised between, —
What would become of me?

(Nay, do not laugh!
To me all this was real.)

My young thoughts caught,
From tone and gesture, something earnest meant
For all of us; there would be some mishap,
Unless we all did something. Restlessly
My small life fluttered in its vast, bare cage,
Yet feared the terror hinted at outside.

And then they sung a hymn, that sometimes was
Squared to the preaching, like a scaffold-stair;

But sometimes lifted up my baby-soul,
And took it heavenward through the apple-bloom,
With birds and winds, and all the free, glad things
That worshipped in unconscious unrestraint, —
As in Thorwaldsen's sculpture, where the babes
Are borne through kingdoms of the Night and Day,
In mighty, motherly embrace.
But when
The words came, "Let us pray!" something in me
Awoke, and understood, and said, "Amen!"
But O the weary failure! That long prayer
Was like a toilsome journey round the world,
By Cathay and the Mountains of the Moon,
To come at our own door-stone, where He stood
Waiting to speak to us, the Father dear,
Who is not far from any one of us.

And yet, though baby-feet flagged in the way,
The hard, cold way of prayer those stern men chose,
Not for one moment did one thought in me
Doubt that there was a way, some path of prayer
By which I, too, could reach Him. And perhaps
The men and women standing up so straight,
With set, unwinking eyes, perhaps their thoughts
Stumbled like mine, sometimes. How could they go,

Step after measured step, as they were led,
Shaping their asking to the preacher's plan,
Without a side-flight of their own ?
                                                            God hears
The prayer the good man means, the soul's desire,
Under whatever rubbish of vain speech.
And prayer is, must be, each man's deepest word.
He who denies its power still uses it
Whenever he names God or thinks of Him.

If there be Better, — and the dream of it,
The longing for it, shows that there must be, —
It is not in ourselves; it is the God
Beyond, whom our souls seek; the search is prayer.
More life we ask, of Him who is the Life :
The reason why we pray is this : we must.

Therefore the breeze of memory brings to me
No sweeter echo than that Sabbath word
From pew and pulpit hid by apple-boughs
Among the years of childhood, "Let us pray!"
And therefore, though Philosophy forbid, —
Philosophy, the soul of whose germ-thought
Is God, the thought-inspirer; — therefore, though
Science forbid, closing the inward eye

To make the outward keener; putting Law,
God's vast, revealing shadow, for himself, —
Still let the instinct of his presence speak,
That will take no denial; still let heart
Respond to heart, — deep calling unto deep,
The voice of many waters, — "Let us pray!"

VI.

WEEKS passed : and cheerful mornings dawned on Ruth
Out of her girl-friends' eyes. To hearts like hers,
Sick for a little kindness, just the sound
Of sympathetic voices brings relief.

Some strangers came one day into the mills, —
Among them English travellers, — led on
Through the great labyrinth of dust and noise
By the good Superintendent, — a grave man,
Kindly and manly, and esteemed of all.

They paused awhile among the balsam-flowers
And pinks and marigolds about the gate ;
Then peered with curious eyes through every door
Along the winding stair. The carding-room
They gave one glance, with its great groaning wheels,
Its earthquake rumblings, and its mingled smells
Of oily suffocation ; and passed on

Into another room's cool spaciousness
Of long clean alleys, where the spinners paced
Silently up and down, and pieced their threads,
The spindles buzzing like ten thousand bees.

Two bright-faced little girls looked up and smiled,
Swinging a bobbin-box between them. These
Were Ann and Alice, who, in April, played
Beside Pawtucket Falls. One stranger said, —

" Now, sir, this should not be! You 're copying
Our British faults too closely, when a child
Toils in close air, like this." But carelessly
The children laughed, still turning work to play,
As children will, nor hardship's meaning guessed.

The next great door swung in upon a room
Where the long threads were wound from beam to beam,
And glazed, and then fanned dry in breathless heat.
Here lithe forms reached across wide webs, or stooped
To disentangle broken threads, or climbed
To where their countenances glistened pale
Among swift belts and pulleys, which appeared
To glow with eyes, like the mysterious wheels

Seen of Ezekiel once, by Chebar's brook.
Ruth Woodburn's earnest, too unsmiling face
Was one of these, arresting soon the gaze
Of those who entered.
"That 's a striking brow;
An intellectual girl, you may be sure,"
One to another said. "Who is she, sir?"

"I knew her father well, — a man of gifts,
But not of faculty; dead now. She 's here
To save the homestead, and help educate
Brothers and sisters. She will do it, too.
She is continually anxious for more work,
More than her strength will bear, I fear. But then
These young girls every day astonish me
By some such aim's accomplishment."
"I wish
She had an easier life: she looks too sad
And grave and worn-out, — homesick, I am sure;
And this room's heat must undermine her strength."

The good man's brow grew serious. "If, being here,
I needs must solve all problems of these lives, —
A hopeless task, — perplexed I must withdraw

And seek a wiser man to fill my place.
But work 's a blessed curse, and some of these
Would wonder at our pity; smile, perhaps."
And so he led them to the weaving-room.

The door, swung in on iron hinges, showed
A hundred girls who hurried to and fro,
With hands and eyes following the shuttle's flight,
Threading it, watching for the scarlet mark
That came up in the web, to show how fast
Their work was speeding. Clatter went the looms,
Click-clack the shuttles. Gossamery motes
Thickened the sunbeams into golden bars,
And in a misty maze those girlish forms,
Arms, hands, and heads, moved with the moving looms,
That closed them in as if all were one shape,
One motion. For the most part tidy they,
And comely; wholesome-looking country girls.
But now and then a stolid face, an eye
That held a covetous glint, a close, cold mouth,
Made emphasis for itself. And now and then
A countenance eloquent with quiet thought
And noble aspiration, shone out clear,
A sun amid the cloud-like nebulæ.

Here Esther, Eleanor, and Isabel
Worked in a sunlit corner, side by side,
That looked down towards the river.
Eleanor's plants, —
Roses, and one great oleander-tree, —
Blooming against the panes, intensified
The whiteness of her face. Across to her
Leaned Isabel with a startled look.
" My looms, —
Tend them five minutes, will you?" And she slipped
Behind some piled-up webs, and, crouching there,
With bowed head, seemed intent upon a heap
Of untrimmed cloth; there lingering, until
The strangers disappeared. Then she returned,
Resuming work in silence; not unmissed.

The Superintendent had drawn near, and said
Aside, to one guest, " I will show you now
A maiden worthy of Murillo's brush.
But no! she is not here. That pale-faced girl
Does double work for her. However, there
Is Esther Hale; a soul more generous
I know not among women. She will work
All day, and watch beside the sick all night,
If need be, and she covers the mistakes

Of clumsy learners, till they mend. Indeed,
Her virtues lean toward faults sometimes, for she
Is quite too careless of her own health, goes
To meeting in all weathers, has a class
Of children at the Sunday school, and finds,
Somehow or other, time to visit them,
And know them well. I own that I have felt
Like scolding her, when I have seen her give
Her bank-notes to build churches, or perhaps
Fill up the missionary-box. She well
Deserves to wed a Prince — or President."

"Or choose a better portion, with Saint Paul,
And be a woman-saint." The lady spoke,
Scarce knowing that she did; whereat all laughed,
And so went out.
A sunbeam at the door
Fixed one man's face an instant: Eleanor knew
That face; it was the stranger's at the bridge!
Was it from his eyes Isabel hid herself?
Who was he? And what meant this mystery
Of conscious looks and blushes? Isabel
She could not question; Esther was forbidden.
But into Eleanor's soul there came a sense
Of anxious guardianship.

"I shall be shown
The way to help her, if she needs my help,"
She told herself, yet resolutely set
Her thoughts to seeking clews; for much she feared
Some snare was near the footsteps of her friend.

The shuttles clattered on. The red rose leaned
Out toward the wonder of the open sky;
And Eleanor leaned out too, and longed for light
That souls might see by. Bending then again
Over her work, she spread a little book
Open, beneath a warp-fringe from her loom, —
A book of hymns she loved; and as she toiled,
Her voice made music, hid within the noise, —
A bird's note in a thicket; and her heart
Rose, with her voice, in singing that was prayer.

Heavenly Helper, Friend divine,
Friend of all men, therefore mine,
Let my heart as thy heart be!
Breathe thy living breath through me!

Only at thy love's pure tide
Human thirst is satisfied.
He who fills his chalice there
Fills, with thirstier souls to share.

Undefiled One, who dost win
All thine own from paths of sin,
Never let me dread to go
Where is guilt, or want, or woe!

If another lose the way,
My feet also go astray.
Sleepless Watcher, lead us back,
Safe into the homeward track!

As a bird unto its nest,
Flies the tired soul to thy breast.
Let not one an alien be!
Lord, we have no home but Thee!

VII.

Ruth Woodburn sat alone in her own room;
A most unusual privilege, — her own, —
Hers only, — seven feet square! With Esther Hale
For house-companion, she was well content.

It was midsummer now: the crickets chirped
Along green-fringed canals and through trim yards;
And one had somehow climbed the bricks, and hid
His black limbs somewhere, just to sing to her.

And Ruth could sing herself, with pen and ink.
She soothed her heartaches so, sometimes; though close
She hid her old portfolio full of verse, —
All sentiment, she knew; but only thus
Would grief translate the blurred text of chained books
In her heart's crypt.

'T is no good place for songs,
Dungeoned in self. Birds in a darkened cage
Stop singing: a true hymn is born of light.
Still Ruth won some poor comfort from her grief,
Humming it over to herself alone,
Half hopeful of its taking wing at last.

CAN you do without me?
Is the summer just as sweet
With its grass untroubled
By my once familiar feet?
Does the west-wind never
Stir the woodland with a sigh
For a presence missing,
Once the dearest that drew nigh?

Can you do without me?
Is it all the same to be
Living with a silence,
Gulf-like, stretched from you to me?
If you can, so be it!
God has weighed our mutual need:
He appoints our places;
Sways the thought, permits the deed.

You can do without me,
  And without you I live on,
Wedded to grave duty;
  Feet must walk, when wings are gone.
Lost the cup's aroma,
  All that freshens and uplifts;
Faded out, the vision
  From the gray horizon drifts.

If I loved a phantom, —
  If it filled my atmosphere
With a dream's illusion, —
  In the unrevealed, so near,
Dreams may be made real:
  There the true soul I may know,
Yours has but foreshadowed:
  So God bless you, as you go!

A step was on the stair; and Esther's hand
Touched now the latch. Ruth laid the paper by,
But its thought lingered in her eyes, and ran
Into her words, despite herself.
                                        "Sit here,
Where you can see the tree-tops and the sky,

So many yards of sheeny blue, all mine!
I never say my prayers but I thank God
That I have this, instead of staring rows
Of windows in brick walls. Only to think
Of a time come to me when loneliness
And that one sky-strip seem like luxury!
But I have room-mates plenty: crowds of thoughts,
Not always kind or smiling.

"Esther dear,
I never told, you never asked of me, —
For that I thank you, — what the trouble is
Which I have worn, like mourning, ever since
A stranger, sick, you found and took me in.
Have you the patience now to hear of it?"

"Aught that concerns you, Ruth, comes home to me;
But telling may be too great pain."

"Relief,
Dear friend, it will be now, though once I hoped
To hide me with my sorrow in the grave.
But you will think me foolish, to have cared
For one man so that memory of him
Clouds life all over. Think me so! I am.
Owning it folly, I can talk of it.

If I can make a weary story brief,
I 'll tell you of a teacher that I had.
Winter on winter, when the frozen hills
Were white ghost-giants round us, when the snow
Buried us up like Laplanders, he came,
And with old Virgil, made an Italy
Of cold New Hampshire. I, beyond the rest,
Prizing the Latin lore, we studied much
Together, in long evenings, by ourselves.
And all the bright vacations, side by side,
We wandered with the west-wind through the hills.

"To me he told his plans. His college years
Once finished, he would settle at the West,
As rovers settle, — teach, or preach, perhaps;
'Might I not join him, some time?' And it seemed,
At last, the only natural thing to dream
That we should have one future.

"So I lived,
Of that great garden-desert picturing
A home for us two.

"When my father died,
New cares fell on me. With her mortgaged farm
And her large family, my mother's head,
Never too clear, seemed utterly confused.

I shelved my books. I set the boys to work,
And kept a strict account of costs.
"In vain!
The two ends would not meet. Friends offered help
I was too proud to take. I heard of those
Who here had found the wherewithal to lift
Loads heavier than mine. So I came, too,
Full of my Eden-visions about work,
With the curse lifted off, and full of hope
For Ambrose and our prairie-paradise:
Not his, not mine, but ours!
"Well, he I loved —
And love still, with a difference — had gone
Part way upon his journey, sending words
Of old accustomed tenderness to me. —
I think he meant them; men are very strange. —
He met my cousin somewhere on the road,
Whom he had never seen, sweet Zillah Wray,
Bewitching as May dawns or mountain-brooks.
They talked of me. 'She was so fond of me,
I was so good, so true, so lovable,
And knew so much, withal!' O, I can hear
Just how she said it, with an innocent air
Of self-depreciation! 'What was she
But a mere ignoramus?' And the word

Rounded her lips so prettily, one sighed
To kiss them. 'Still, she never had been taught
As Ruth had. Did he think that she could learn?'

"So Ambrose, lingering in her native town,
Called on her often, — for my sake, he said;
And taught her — not so much as she taught him.
He learned to love her; and he wrote to me,
Making confession. 'Could they help their fate,
Their mutual fault? Could I forgive them both?
He doubted — Zillah was so different,
Seemed so much fonder of him — if I cared
Greatly to share his wandering destinies.'

"That was the penalty of reticence!
Love, I had thought, was treasure men should seek,
And prize the more, being hid. It is not so! —
Foolish Cordelia should have answered Lear! —
Man likes the false wind's wooing, wants bold flowers
To bring him incense; so much trouble saved!

"Though crushed, I was not wholly unprepared,
For I remembered Zillah. Like a dress,
Becoming, and so kept in wearing trim,
Was this unconscious show of artlessness.

Her guileful guilelessness seemed natural
As life itself. Yet Ambrose, I supposed,
Had penetration to read her and me.
It was like death to me, untwisting all
The fibres of my life from his, and still
In memory painful. But he is not mine,
Or she could not have won him. I have tried
To think with gratitude of her bright ways,
And how she will adorn his life; and yet
He seemed to need me, as I needed him.
And Zillah loves — perhaps I do her wrong —
Herself reflected in the heart she wins,
More than the man she won."

"And," Esther said,
"Perhaps your Ambrose also loves himself
Glassed in her admiration. Wisest men
Lose all their wisdom when a silly girl
Cobwebs their ears with flattery. To my mind,
'T is fancy's glamour, both sides; never love."

"So I have almost thought, else were my past
With him I loved a sealed-up sepulchre
Wet by no tear of memory. But sometimes
I dream of him bewildered, shaken off
By Zillah, when she scents superior game,

Conscious of his mistake, and missing me;
Or, wedding her, hindered in all his best
For want of wifely help, and missing me.
Try as I will, the thought of him comes back,
With Zillah or without her, missing me,
Who never can return."

"How never, Ruth?
May not all rents be mended?"

"Not of souls.
Mine, surely, will not wear a patched-up love,
Nor such as can be worn by me or her,
At change of the giver's fancy. Even now
I dimly see why disappointment came,
To lead me upward to some grander height
Of hope and labor. Still the grinding wheels
Crush on, the red drops ooze. The Juggernaut,
Experience, never heeds its victim's cry."

"Your Ambrose was not worthy of you, Ruth."

"Nay, that I do not know. Men cannot help
Being drawn aside by beauty."

"Can they not?
Poor weaklings! Why do women call them 'lords,'
Who are not their own masters? I should scorn
The man mere pretty faces could enslave."

"You know not what you talk of, Esther dear!
A woman's heart is as perversely fixed
As man's is wavering. Some day, for yourself
You may see how it is: I hope not soon."

"Never! My thoughts are shut fast, marriage-ward.
There is much else to live for; full as much
For woman as for man, in separateness:
Although my dream is, that the two, made one
In mutual faith, show Paradise as yet
An earthly possibility. But then
You say, dear Ruth, you never can return
To Ambrose, yet must love him. That is strange!"

"Yes, it is strange; and sad as it is strange,
And true as strange and sad. I think of him
As a wife death has summoned, who may look
Backward from heaven, and love her husband still
For the last smile he gave her, though his smiles
Are now another woman's sunshine. She
Whom he has seen safe through the gates of pearl,
Cannot go back with him across the gulf
His thoughts make, widening towards new marriage.
"Well!
My story told, let 's find some cheerier talk!"

And here came Isabel's rosy, roguish face
Half through the doorway: "Esther, there are guests
Waiting to see you, — gentlemen": and ran,
Without another word, they knew not where.

Esther had on her working-dress, a print
Somewhat the dimmer for much washing, still
Tidy enough. She only smoothed her hair
By Ruth's six-square-inch mirror, then went down;
And who should wait there in the dining-room,
Which served for evening sittings, — sewing, talk,
And reading going on among the girls,
A dozen of them, scattered round the room,
At the bare tables, — who but Doctor Mann
And Pastor Alwyn, with them Eleanor,
Serene and ladylike, in easy chat?

Somewhat constrained, vexed that she was abashed
To meet a cultured stranger in the place
Where her lot fell, so different from his, —
Esther talked rapidly, unlike herself,
While Eleanor and her physician-friend
Went rambling through long genealogies.

A pedlar came in while they stayed, whose wares
The girls sat cheapening. A phrenologist
Displaced the pedlar, and a tide of mirth
Flowed in around the tables, as he read
The cranial character of each to each.

The guests arose to go, one much annoyed, —
The kindly Pastor, who had seldom found
Things so untoward, even in a boarding-house.
But Eleanor and young Doctor Mann had gone
Back under haunted boughs of family-trees,
Nor heard near voices. Dim shapes of the past,
Moving before them, all at hand obscured;
And he remembered but her gentle face.

Esther escaped to her third-story room,
Glad that her mates were absent, — sought the nook
She called her own, a space between the bed
And window, wide enough to hold one chair,
Where she could see the stars, unjostled, move
Across the open sky-fields. Room! more room!
Her thoughts cried out for. So to live, so cramped
As not to hear your nearest neighbor's voice
Through the surrounding jargon, was it life?
But here she was, — must make the best of it,

Till a new door should open. Even now
It swung upon its hinges, all unheard
By her. If we could watch the bursting gates
Of Destiny, should we not shrink back, awed
By their vast shadow, dazed with light beyond?
Man's eye suits his horizon. As that spreads,
Vision grows telescopic, till, beside
The throne of God, it sweeps eternity.

Meanwhile Ruth Woodburn sat uncomforted
Beneath the thickening stars; nor could she guess
That her young hopes, now beaten down like grass
Under a furious rain, would rise again
With greener vigor for that cleansing storm.

God made not any human life to rest
Only upon another human life:
Love means some better thing than that. And she
Who so had leaned upon a man she loved,
Found her dependence weakness, and not need,
Ere autumn waned. Before her heart wore off
Its rust of sorrow, and long afterward,
Through its vibrations, chords like this awoke:—

Once 't was my saddest thought,
Ere I began to doubt you,

That some time I must learn,
  Perhaps, to do without you.
For Death parts dearest friends;
  From him there 's no escaping;
And partings worse than death
  Our fears are ever shaping.

Now with new dawns of hope
  No thought of you is blended;
Day deepens evermore,
  Though morning dreams are ended.
And now the saddest thought
  That haunts my heart about you
Is this, — that I have learned,
  At last, to do without you.

VIII.

"Good by, girls! I am homeward bound. To-night
I shall nod back Chocorua's welcome. Girls,
They talk of strikes, — they say that half the looms
Must stop, or wages be reduced. A muss
Of some kind will be stirring. So get leave
To come, and, till it settles, rest with me.
Come! I 'm in earnest."
Minta Summerfield
Stood in her cottage-bonnet and bright shawl
Outside the door, just as the bell rang in
The girls from half-hour breakfasting. They gave
Hurried replies, half-promises. The coach
Rolled out of sight. The summer seemed to go
With Minta's breezy laughter from their side;
Might they not follow?
Eleanor demurred,
Because of Isabel left behind. "But Ruth,

Ruth will be with her; each will care for each;
And Isabel loves Ruth, and Ruth is kind."

So Esther, in her cheerful way, went on
Planning the journey; and before aware,
They found themselves inhaling the fresh breath
Of the hill-country, from the stage-coach top.

O that first burst of beauty from the shore
Of Winnepesaukee, where the mountains lay
Floating, a chain of ever-varying pearls
In shifting light and shadow! It was like
The Book of Revelation, Esther said;
The vision of a new heaven and new earth;
Gleams of the Bride's celestial jewelry,
From the white City of God. But Eleanor
Sat still, as one entranced, her dove-like eyes
Filled with unutterable light.
They stayed
An evening and a morning by the Lake,
Among the tangled sweet-briers of the steep,
Where, sitting upon fern-wreathed rocks, they saw
The low sun redden against Ossipee,
The white moon's shadow drift like a canoe
Among innumerable islands green;

And all the water's glory, fading, blend
At last into one wavering spectacle,
Commingling islands, billows, hills, and sky.

Then, after next day's noon-glare, they went up
For nearer greeting of the hills; and saw,
Through veils of rain, green summits come and go;
And saw a lucent rainbow, laid against
A mountain's purple slope, clear and intense
With unadulterate color; and at last
The landscape was all mountains. The whole range
Rose near and dark, its grand horizon-lines
Cut on the northern sky from east to west,
Like the long swell of an oncoming wave
Stiffened to granite ere it broke. Vast clouds
Moving to eastward in slow cavalcade
Now hid and now revealed one lofty peak
Whose white head, worn and haggard with the storms
Of æons, held its mighty symmetry
Amid surrounding chaos.
The two girls,
Who best knew mountains glimpsed among the leaves
Of the Old Testament, seemed to behold
The glooms of Sinai! Esther told her thought
To Eleanor, who whispered back, "The Lord

Is in His holy temple; let us keep
Silence before Him." So they fared along
To a broad, well-tilled upland, whence the hills
More smiling looked, amid brown pasture-lands
And pleasant farm-enclosures, neighborly
As sentinels who keep no dangerous watch.

The coach stopped. From a roadside cottage-porch,
Wreathed with convolvulus, out flew a form
Familiar. "Welcome!" Minta Summerfield
Called, with a clap of hands. "Come in! come in!
You are not used to rough-and-tumble roads.
Poor wayfarers! I hope your bones are sound!"

The days that followed, in and out of doors,
With best home-cheer, and still fresh pages turned
Of wonder and of beauty, everywhere
The sun could lay his finger, — light of light
On the receding and advancing hills,
The sweet air like a flagon of new wine
Freshening their senses, wakening fantasies
That heretofore slept dreamless, making life
Seem nobler, better, dearer than itself, —
Those days were treasure which no flimsy wealth
Of words could represent. To some new world
They seemed translated.

Here was Minta's home
With her tall farmer-brother, Clement, who,
Had won a wife as sweet as he deserved,
A steady-natured and wise-hearted one,
Who toiled with him, not holding work the end
Of their joint life, but kept a margin clear
For studious thought, for books, for all that helped
The mother and the woman to be true;
So broadening, as she could, their rustic lot.

Sisters in love as well as law, the two,
Mercy and Minta, homely labors shared,
And simple joys, and cheerfulness of health.
And pleasant was the long ride home from school
Over the windings of the Tamworth hills,
After each week of absence, when they came,
Clement and Mercy, with two sunburnt boys, —
Cupids in bronze, till winter showed fair brows
And rosy apple-cheeks by fireside light,
Like Raphael's cherubs, — when the happy four
Came in the old farm-wagon, the white horse
Jogging on slowly for the landscape's sake,
Or the good company he bore, and took
Minta's gay presence back with them, to bloom
Into their Sabbath-Siloam of peace.

The schoolhouse door was closed now, and the girls
Drove the white Wizard anywhere they would,
The faithful beast by Esther named, because
He bore them always through enchanted ground;
So seemed the mountains to her fancy, bred
Beside the gray-blue level of the sea,
And grassy borders of the Merrimack.

One day they reached an inn upon a knoll
At noontide, hungering and tired, and there
For the good Wizard's welfare and their own,
They rested. In the low-ceiled dining-room,
Among the lingerers of the summer, sat
A lovely gray-haired woman, whose mild eyes
Looked welcome, and who led them with kind words,
After their meal, out under sheltering elms,
Where they could see strange peaks, invisible
From the home-cottage, ten good miles away.

In that sweet woman-stranger's heart sprang up
For Eleanor a secret tenderness.
Her she besought to stay, so pale she looked,
So long the journey home. And Esther, too,
Blaming herself for Eleanor's fatigue,
Added her urging. Eleanor yielded then,

And let the Wizard bear her friends away,
Looking and listening till his distant hoofs
Fell light as raindrops; then, half homesick, moaned.

But she was met by thoughtfulness too kind
To be resisted. Miriam Willoughby,
A single woman with a mother's heart
Such as too many a child cries after, mocked
By the empty mother-name, knew just what word
To whisper, what soft silence to enfold
About the maid, and she was comforted.

And when, at dawn, slow vapors climbed the hills
Before the pleasant hostelry, and left
Crags of dark green contrasted with pure blue,
These new-made friends beheld the mountains play
Like dolphins in their sun-bath, with the clouds
That clung to them, or slipped off unaware
Into a sea of azure, drenching them
With half-concealing sheen. And presently
The elder woman called, "Look! Eleanor, look!"
And where her finger pointed, where the mists
Had fallen again, and left the whole world gray
As if with coming rain, far, far beyond
The wave-like outline of the mountain-range,

A sun-touched summit glistened, a great pearl
Held in a cup-like hollow of near hills
Dark with contrasted glory.
"O, too fair!
Too delicate to gaze or breathe upon!
Is it not heaven itself?" And Eleanor's eyes
Grew luminous as she looked.
A veil came down
Upon the vision. Miriam Willoughby
Took Eleanor's hand, and said, "'T was but a hill
Like these around us, but a little higher, —
Although crowned monarch of New England peaks.
And may not heaven itself be common life
In uttermost perfection? Such a glimpse
Comes now and then to us from human souls,
Lit with divine ideas and purposes.
Is not man as the angels, only made
A little lower? And who knows what shall be
Revealed in him, shone on by other suns?"

The mist became a rainfall, and that day
No Esther came, so the two women sat
And wound their friendship firm with genial talk
Each of the other's welfare, and of things
Wherein they found their aspirations blend.

For though this Miriam Willoughby had place
In high society, nor toiled nor spun
More than the lilies, with her lily hands
Still as unwrinkled as her face, while snows
Of threescore years had whitened on her head,
Her heart and brain held a whole lifetime full
Of sympathy and generous help, nor once
Allowed the thought that fortune, gifts, or birth,
Privileged arrogance, or permitted scorn
Of any toiler in the human hive.

The years had dwelt with her most peacefully,
Each one a guest more welcome than the last;
And why the ripening of her days should be
Clouded with vain regrets for blossom-time,
As with some women, she had seen no cause,
With autumn in her heart surpassing spring
In subtle fragrance and perennial bloom.
Yet motherhood, a fountain sealed within,
Sometimes made lonesome music, and she longed
For those who needed her caress, her close
And separate overwatch of yearning care.

All orphanage awoke her love; but now
This Eleanor, who toiled for daily bread,

In her pale beauty, fragile unto pain,
Seemed to glide in and fill the emptiest nook
Of her warm heart, that echoed, "Mine! my child!"

A feeling near akin to jealousy
She recognized when Esther came at last,
So waited for by Eleanor; but, ashamed
Before itself, her heart gave room to both;
And days and days she kept them at her side,
Growing to them most dear. The roadside inn
Was homelike, and the three friends went and came,
Together or alone, free as the breeze
That rippled Bearcamp Water.

As she watched
The two girls wandering down the meadow-road,
One golden morning, Miriam Willoughby
Sat at her window, and, in pauses, wrote
To one who shared her passion for the hills: —

"Dear Nephew Ralph, it often seems to me
As if we should change places. 'T is not fair
That you should toil in the metropolis
At stifling office-work, at my affairs
More than your own, I fear, while I enjoy
Perpetual leisure, drinking peace and health

Out of the mountain chalices. For you
'T is hard, who Nature as a mother love,
As you do me, your old,rom antic aunt,
Whose heart remains a girl's in loving you,
Her squire and champion. We 'll let business go,
While I write of these hills, at your desire, —
The friendly hills, that, while I am away
From all I love, must take the place of friends.

" This mountain-group, before my window ranged,
Is noble company to have in sight,
To sit down with at any hour of day, —
To meet their faces looking toward the east
At the sunrising, wrapped in soft noon-mist,
Or outlined keen upon the auroral night,
Or sinking into sunset deeps of heaven,
Unutterably glorious. Yet sometimes,
As one may weary of too great a throng
Of noble guests, and call them each apart
For closer conference, I move my seat
Little by little, so that only one
Is for the time in sight.

" Green Ossipee,
With Bearcamp River singing at its base,
A vast, long-terraced wall of fir and pine,

Shuts in our southern meadows. Where that ends,
Just where the sun sets in October days,
Mount Israel stands and guards his villages,
And hides the secret of a windy pass
To Thornton, and the Haystacks of the Notch.

"Then the eye rests upon Black Mountain's top
Of sombre velvet, highest of these hills,
That gathers the rich purple and deep gold
Of fine late light into his vesture's folds,
Yet, in his rounded symmetry, appears
Less grand than Whiteface, his next-neighbor peak,
Looking, sharp-cut and gray, out of the north,
With outreach of bare shoulder; in his side
A gash deep-hollowed, where the sun at noon
Pours clearest oil and wine.

"Some sonneteer,
Travelling this way, has hung a little web
Of misty melody about his brow.
Travelling this way, he must have wandered on
Over steep roads of Sandwich, when he wrote
Of Whiteface as a monarch whom the clouds
Gather toward, wingèd daughters of the sky, —
For of this vale Chocorua is king.

CLOUDS ON WHITEFACE.

So lovingly the clouds caress his head, —
  The mountain-monarch ; he, severe and hard,
  With white face set like flint horizon-ward ;
They weaving softest fleece of gold and red,
And gossamer of airiest silver thread,
  To wrap his form, wind-beaten, thunder-scarred.
They linger tenderly, and fain would stay,
Since he, earth-rooted, may not float away.
  He upward looks, but moves not ; wears their hues ;
Draws them unto himself ; their beauty shares ;
  And sometimes his own semblance seems to lose,
  His grandeur and their grace so interfuse ;
And when his angels leave him unawares,
A sullen rock, his brow to heaven he bares.

"'T is curious, Ralph, the naming of these hills, —
Black Mountain from his dark pine-growth ; and this
From his vast, perpendicular front of quartz
Cutting the sky, a wedge of adamant.
'White,' 'Black,' 'Green,' 'Blue,' were obviously conferred
Out of the settlers' poverty ; worse taste

Was theirs who threw pell-mell on Agiochook
A shower of Presidential surnames. Yet,
Why nickname all this grandeur? 'Ragged,' 'Bald,'
'Toad,' 'Snout,' and 'Hunchback,'— so you hear them called
Among the farmers roundabout.

"One day
We went out on a christening-tour, two girls
And I; we said the red man should receive
His own again, and with Chocorua
And Passaconaway, should Paugus stand.
That crouching shape, a headless heap afar,
Glittering as if with barbarous ornaments,
Suits well the sachem whose wild howl resounds
Through history like the war-whoop of the wind.
And all that craggy chaos at his side
Shall be the Wahwa Hills, for the grim chief
Who after Paugus trails uncertainty
Of blood-stained memory, in dim ruin lost.
And that bright cone of perfect emerald
Whose trout-streams flow through birchen intervales,—
An angler's Paradise,— that shall be called
For Wannalancet, peacefullest of all
The forest sagamores, the one who loved
The white man best, found him most treacherous.

"The mighty name of Passaconaway,
Honored of all his tribe, and honored too
Of pioneers, with whom he held firm truce,
Life-long, rests fitly on yon pyramid
Of stately greenness. Were he sorcerer
Or not, he is a cloud-compeller still.

"Beside him leans Chocorua from his hold,
With the curse stiffened on his silent lips,
Gazing upon the shadow of himself
In his lake-mirror. Nobly picturesque
Is ragged, legend-wrapped Chocorua,
Leader of this long file of mountain-shapes,
Most human-seeming in his sharp contours.

Here is a picture of him, from the same
Stray rhymer's pencil, showing possible moods
Of this most moody mountain-sagamore,
Who, savage as he is, knows how to smile.

CHOCORUA.

THE pioneer of a great company
That wait behind him, gazing toward the east, —
Mighty ones all, down to the nameless least, —

Though after him none dares to press, where he
With bent head listens to the minstrelsy
 Of far waves chanting to the moon, their priest.
 What phantom rises up from winds deceased?
What whiteness of the unapproachable sea?
 Hoary Chocorua guards his mystery well:
He pushes back his fellows, lest they hear
 The haunting secret he apart must tell
To his lone self, in the sky-silence clear.
A shadowy, cloud-cloaked wraith, with shoulders bowed,
He steals, conspicuous, from the mountain-crowd.

"Yet, Ralph, the noblest landscape was but meant
To be a background for humanity.
And these two girls, — you need not be afraid
(I know the shyness of your bachelor-heart)
Of two young mill-girls, — ladies, both of them,
As I translate the word, — will go away,
Only too soon, will leave me quite alone;
And loneliness after good company
Is not the bearable sort.

"Do not forget
To speak of Rodney when you write. Poor boy!
Brother so unlike you! If he could feel

The baptism of one work-day's honest sweat,
Happy for him! To wear his idleness
As gracefully as the last cut of coat
Seems his life's end and purpose.

"Nephew Ralph,
Be idle just one week yourself! for here
I and the mountains wait and hope for you!"

IX.

Some faces stand for twilight, or the shade
Of web-like dog-day mist, which does but wrap
Summer-flushed earth in a becoming veil;
These have a fascination of their own:
But when a face which is the sun itself
Wears an eclipse, sad for the world it lights!

Something was strange at Clement Summerfield's,
And that was Minta's countenance, now vexed
With knots, and puzzling twists of lip and brow;
Now gazing vague defiance into air;
And now at war with tears, but conquering.

Her guests seemed her chief pleasure, and they knew
It was no sorrow to her that their stay
Caused rarer visits from a farmer's son
Bred just across the mountain, who had found
Excuse of trade, or work exchanged, to come

Often to Clement's cottage, and stay long;
Minta's "Perhaps," — the household cognomen
When he was out of hearing; and in months
Gone by, referred to as "The Probable."
But Solon Dale, whatever he had been
To Minta, was not now what he would be, —
Accepted suitor, — yet was unconvinced
That hence their paths inevitably diverged,
And never could make one road, — that being his.

It was a first-love fallacy, perceived
As such by Minta, every day made clear
By her whole nature's undisguised revolt
From his accustomed mastery of will,
And narrow, obstinate plan, that tethered her
To the obsolete letter of a promise dead.

Moreover, mountain-high he piled the wall
Betwixt them, scoffing at her taste for books,
Which spoilt her for a housewife. Well enough
For those two white-faced friends of hers, he said, —
Spinsters elect; but what a farmer's wife
Wanted of more than just to read and write,
And cipher through the Long Division rules,
He could not see! To teach the district school

No more was needed. Learned she could not be, —
It was not in her.

"Which last may be true,
But I reserve right to be my own judge,"
Thought Minta; and grew sure that Solon's self
Would be the one most uninteresting book
To take for life-long conning. Yet sometimes
Memories of ancient fondness would awake
And counterfeit love's claim. And so things stood
When Esther went to Eleanor at the inn.
And Esther, wishing much, for Minta's peace,
That she would say the unavoidable "No"
For once and always in their absence, stayed
To give her solitude and unbiassed thought.

Letters from Ruth came often. Isabel
And she were quiet, 'mid continual stir
Of work-and-wages questions. There had been
Meetings, conventions; now and then a girl
Spoke on the rostrum for herself, and such
As felt aggrieved. Ruth did not like that course,
Nor "strikes," that ever threatened. "Why should we,
Battling oppression, tyrants be ourselves,
Forcing mere brief concession to our wish?

Are not employers human as employed?
Are not our interests common? If they grind
And cheat as brethren should not, let us go
Back to the music of the spinning-wheel,
And clothe ourselves at hand-looms of our own,
As did our grandmothers. The very name
Of 'strike' has so unwomanly a sound,
If not inhuman, savoring of old feuds
And savage conflicts! If indeed there is
Injustice, — if the rule of selfishness
Must be, invariably, mill-owners' law,
As the dissatisfied say, — if evermore
The laborer's hire tends downward, then we all
Must elsewhere turn; for nobody should moil
Just to add wealth to men already rich.
Only a drudge will toil on, with no hope
Widening from well-paid labor."

So Ruth thought
And wrote to Esther. And of Isabel, —
For Eleanor's anxious fears would not be hid,
And Ruth had been close questioned, —

"Isabel
Seemed never happier; no, nor handsomer!
She is so like the fragrant blush-rose buds
That looked in from the garden, when the days

Were long in June, and I was at my book
Or sewing in my favorite doorway-seat,
My father still alive, and all things glad!
I love her for her beauty, and she seems
To bring back the lost perfume of my youth."

And Miriam Willoughby, let in to all
The interests of these two, persuaded them,
Now that her Ralph sent word of new delays
And complications not to be escaped,
To be her guests awhile, and they explored
Together the hill-country.
Lakes that held
Great mountain-mysteries in their bosoms, stilled
With wonder, or moved quietly at times
With ripples as with thoughts, drew their charmed
feet
To white, sequestered beaches. And sometimes
A steady oarsman rowed them down the curves
Of Bearcamp Water to Lake Ossipee,
Whence they returned with spoil of autumn woods,
With trailing streamers, orange, crimson, gold,
Splashing the sombre shadows of the hills
Gloomed in clear crystal; and their little boat
Laden with pine-cones for an evening fire,

Now often welcome, — and with curious flints,
Stone-arrows, dropped by savage Pennacook
Returning on his war-path by the lake,
To the stronghold of Paugus, which they saw
Rise like a dome among the farther hills.

And Miriam told them, sitting side by side
On Ossipee's steep crags, the higher range
Stretching in panorama east and west
Beyond green Bearcamp Valley at their feet, —
No lovelier was Tempe to the Greek, —
Told them how once upon Pequawket's slope
She lingered, as the summer sun went down,
Her fellow-pilgrims vanishing from sight,
Bounding like chamois up into the mists
Of the veiled summit : all the world below,
Path, mountain-forest, changed to one gray blank ;
And she alone there in a vapor-rift,
That left one lichened crag, one blasted tree
Above her head, and one vast mountain-gap
Brimmed with a cloudy sunset's awful red.
That lurid gorge seemed widening vast and far
As an eternity : it was like death,
The silence, and the weight of weariness
That bound her there, immovable ; — when, hark !

An accent almost human overhead, —
Was it indeed a bird? —
"Here, heavenward!
O, here, traveller! heavenward!" —
It sounded as a voice might, dropped to earth
By an ascending seraph. And she said,
"Children, when people talk of nightingales
And skylarks of Old England, you may say
One songster haunts our mountain-solitudes
Whose voice is like a spirit's, never heard
Except as floating from invisible height: —
Though but a sparrow with a snowy throat,
To me it was as if the mountain's heart
Uttered heaven's invitation.
"Yet that night
Was ghostly, more than heavenly; for we stayed
Till dawn upon Pequawket's hidden top,
Hidden from eyes below, that only saw
Our camp-fire as a star above the cloud.
We to ourselves were shipwrecked mariners
In a great sea of pallid mist, that surged
And curled up to our feet. We stood on rocks
Floating in vapor. Dim isles loomed around
Out of the fog, an archipelago
Of desolation. We were cast adrift

'Mid unsubstantial guesses of a world
Such as old Chaos in his slumber shaped.
And some one said, 'We are philosophers!
Life is illusion: we and fogs are real.'
And then another, — with him I agreed, —
'Who climbs to isolation from mankind,
There thinking to find wisdom, is a fool.'"

And then, by magic of her vivid words,
She set their feet among the loftier hills
Peopling the cloudy north. They heard the roar
Of Ammonoosuc; Fabyan's breezy horn,
Wakening the mountain-echoes; saw the trail
Of Ethan Crawford's snow-shoes on the track
Of catamount or bear; and felt the slide
Of the awful avalanche that swept away
The Willey children out of summer sleep,
Through agony of storm and flood, to death,
Knelled by the midnight thunder.
Esther said:
"Better to stay away from those grim heights!
Are not these lower hills more beautiful, —
And grand enough, and terrible enough,
When storms shake their foundations?
"I have learned,

Watching him from the Sandwich upland-fields,
To reverence Whiteface, like a patriarch
Standing up, a head taller than his sons,
Covering them with his mantle. We were housed
At Summerfield Farm one rainy day, a blank
Where once the mountains stood. O, how we longed
To see their faces! All my losses came
Back to me then. Life seemed a sterile plain,
Here and hereafter. Eyes that have climbed steeps
Learn to hate levels. We both sung for joy
When back through a great sunburst came the hills!"

"How grand it was!" said Eleanor. "I have kept
A picture of that mountain-burial
And resurrection; though, Miss Willoughby,
The lines are not my own; I cannot rhyme:—

He stood there, a shape Titanic
  In the midst of the shining range;
Moment by moment his features
  Beamed with some wonderful change:

For the clouds came down out of heaven;
  With light he was robed and crowned,

Till glory exceeded glory
  On the gathering storm around.

They melted to mists of silver;
  That slid like a winding-sheet,
In swathings of shroud-like whiteness,
  From his forehead to his feet.

And then he was seen no longer;
  With the sound of a sobbing rain
The hills withdrew under blackness, —
  A mourning funeral-train.

And amid the vanished mountains
  We sat, through an autumn day,
Remembering the trusted spirits
  Who had passed from sight away;

And knew that their resurrection
  Would be but a veil let down
To show them still in their places,
  Unchangeable, and our own;

And knew that the living who love us,
  Love on, though the mists of doubt

May level our grand horizon,
  And beauty and joy shut out.

And knew — O comforting wonder ! —
  That the mightiest Love of all,
Perceived not, is round about us
  Like an everlasting wall.

So, amid invisible summits,
  We wrapped us in calms of thought.
Faith lulled us to slumber ; and morning
  To life the dead mountains brought.

X.

THE colors of the far hills came and went,
Flushing to rosy purple through soft gray,
As if they heard the voice of Eleanor
And would reply. The gentle girl spoke on:
"I shall not have one memory of pain
To carry hence. That mountain-range is now
Woven, dyed into the texture of my mind;
And, standing at my loom, I shall behold
Its changes making tapestry of the web
My shuttle flies across, so beautiful!
I scarce can call these hills by common names.
They seem like human beings; not dull earth."

"Earth under heavenly veils, transfigured earth,"
Responded Miriam; "God's great messengers,
Prophets anointed, uttering His word.
Draw near to sage or poet, he is man,
Differing from others but in breadth and height,

And power of strange withdrawal into heaven
To win refreshment for the common fields
He lives in, which are life of his own life.
Mountains *are* human, friendly, personal,
And that is why we love them, — fear them, too;
For loftiest human nature holds untamed
Caverns of isolation."

"I shall read
My Wordsworth better now," said Esther; "he,
The poet of the mountains, whom I liked
Least in his long Excursion, hitherto.
It has its flowerless, barren stretches, like
Any bleak mountain-road; but the surprise
Of sunlit peak or crag makes up for aught
Tedious in either; and along the way
Echoes from the deep forests welcome us."

Then Eleanor: "I wish there were no rule
Against our reading in the mills. Sometimes
A line of poetry is such a lift
From the monotonous clatter."

"To the praise
Of mill-girls be the need of such a rule,"
Said Miriam Willoughby. "Far be the time
When no one shall have reason to forbid

Fruit now desired. And yet I wonder much
How you could be obedient."

Esther smiled :
"We are not ; we rebel ; at least, evade.
Few girls but keep some volume hid away
For stealthy reading. Some tear out the leaves
Of an old Bible, and so get the whole ;
For books, not leaves, are tabooed. Others paste
The window-sills with poem, story, sketch :
No one objects to papering bare walls.
I have a memory-book well filled so. There 's
The minstrel of the Merrimack, who sings
For freedom, and is every toiler's friend :
He walks our streets sometimes, and we all know
His 'Yankee Girl,' 'Angel of Patience,' too.
There 's Bryant's 'Thanatopsis,' 'Death of the Flowers,'
Hood's 'Bridge of Sighs,' likewise his 'Song of the Shirt,'
With Shelley's 'Skylark,' Coleridge's 'Mont Blanc.'
These, and more waifs of lovely verse, I 've learned
Between my window and my shuttle's flight.
As well forbid us Yankee girls to breathe
As read ; we cannot help it."

Eleanor smiled :
"One of your favorites, Esther, I 've recalled

Often, among these farms, — about a girl
Who liked a farmer better than a fop, —
And what girl would not? But this poem read
As if the girl had looked down from some height
On working-men, before. Miss Willoughby,
Somehow it vexed our Isabel. And, to stir
Her face into odd, nettled prettiness, —
Pretty even when she 's cross, Esther sometimes
Would make her listen. Esther, say it now!"

HER CHOICE.

STRANGE, strange to herself it seemed for a moment's time, — no more, —
As he turned to smile from his plough in sight of the cottage door,
And she smiled back, and went in under the woodbine leaves,
And sang at her work with the bird that wove a nest in the eaves.

It was not the man of her dreams, out there in his coarse farm-frock,
Sturdy and firm on the earth as a tree or a lichened rock,

With an eye sun-clear in its health, and a cheek red-
bronzed with tan! —
No; that shadow shrank into mist, and fled from this
living man.

She had shaped a pretty ideal, as a child might fash-
ion a doll;
She had clothed him with such perfection as never
Heaven let fall
On the shoulders of mortal wight; but slowly, one
after one,
From her idol fluttered away the shreds by fantasy
spun.

And what of him then was left? There seemed to
scatter in air
An eyebrow's curve, a weak mouth with a delicate
fringe of hair,
And a town-bred curl of contempt for the boors who till
the land. —
She shuddered, to think how empty sometimes is a
wedded hand!

Yet once she had pictured herself that pitiful strip-
ling's bride;
Would have laid her heart on a shrine of a puppet
deified!

For the first commands of the ten all maidens are prone
to break,
In bowing down to such gods as their own crude
fancies make.

And this had been her first love! To her forehead
rushed a flame
As memory taunted and laughed, — the blush of a
matron's shame
At her girlhood's shallowness. Ah! the poets falsely
sing
That the loveliest blossoms of all are gathered in early
spring.

Many a May-day past she had found under leafless
trees
A crowfoot, perhaps, or a tuft of pallid anemones;
Could these compare with the rose, grown shapely in
summer's heat,
Or the lily's late-brimmed cup, or the spice of the
meadow-sweet?

The high sun deepens the scent and color of slow-blown
flowers;
Intense with the white warmth of heaven, glows earth,
in her mid-noon hours.

The more life, richer the love, else life itself is a lie;
And aspiration and faith on the gusts of April die.

And — there the furrow he turned, — her husband, whose cheerful years
Looked out of his eyes with a light that conquered her foolish fears
Of the coming loneliness, when the world would be chill with rime;
Stanch friends and honest were he and his elder field-mate, Time.

And Time, laying by his scythe at their hearth, in the evenings long,
Would read from his ancient scroll, would charm them with noble song.
And life would mellow with love, and the future would open fair
And grand, as the silver of age fell softly upon their hair.

For she had not wedded a clod, whose heart was earthy, of earth,
Whose cattle and acres and crops were the measure of his worth.

He knew the ring of a truth, and the shape of a royal
thought,
And how at integrity's mint the wealth of a land is
wrought.

He labored with mind and strength, and yet he could
wisely rest;
He toiled for his daily bread, and ate it with whole-
some zest
At the world-wide human board, the brother and friend
of all
With whom he could share a hope, on whom let a
blessing fall.

She had chosen a working-man; never idler at heart
was she;
And her possible fate had been the fate of a homesick
bee
In a butterfly's leash, driven on amid scentless and
useless bloom, —
What drudgery were not bliss to inanities of that doom?

Woman's lot at the best is hard; but hardest of all to
share
No growth into larger thought, no struggle, burden,
or prayer.

And again she caught his smile, and silently, proudly
said :
"This man, with the love of my heart and the life of
my soul, I wed."

"A sensible choice ! But farm-life has two sides,"
Said Miriam, "and the wife must share the worst.
Woman's toil is too hard here : she grows old
Before her time. Life's afternoon means rest :
She cannot take it. This ought not to be.
Labor is beautiful : but not too much ;
For that kills beauty in the laborer."

"But labor is not always beautiful.
To much that is distasteful we 're compelled
By circumstances. For our daily bread,
We, who must earn it, have to suffocate
The cry of conscience, sometimes.
"When I 've thought,
Miss Willoughby, what soil the cotton-plant
We weave, is rooted in, what waters it, —
The blood of souls in bondage, — I have felt
That I was sinning against light, to stay
And turn the accursed fibre into cloth

For human wearing. I have hailed one name,
You know it — 'Garrison' — as a slave might hail
His soul's deliverer. Am not I enslaved
In finishing what slavery has begun?"

"And I, dear Esther Hale, in wearing cloth
So rooted, and so woven, am as wrong
As you are. We all share the nation's sin.
The time may come, when with our dearest blood
This blood must be repaid."
"Some other work,"
Said Esther, "many times I 've meant to try:
Housework, for instance: but I could not earn
In that way, aught for others; nor could have
My first wish answered — freedom for my books,
Freedom of my own movements. Every one,
Not wife or daughter, in a land like ours,
Who does much thinking, must prefer to be
Mistress of her own plans; no housemaid can."

"No housemaid, Esther, but the old-time 'help,'—
In our Republic, service means just that,
And all house-masters and house-mistresses
Should hold to that idea, — 'help,' that came
Into a family of ample wealth

And not luxurious tastes, or into one
Less favored, bringing kindness, conscience, strength,
Would be given leisure, would find sympathy,
Also abundant freedom. This has been, —
May be once more—in the millennium!"

The theme drew on their thoughts, and as they talked
They were descending, plucking here and there
A lady-fern, an everlasting-flower,
Or stopping where a rock invited them
To rest, and watch the changes of the hills.
And now they passed into a grove of pines,
Through which the winds were singing.
Up the road
Came Minta and the Wizard. Seeing them,
She left the weary roadster tied, and drew
Into their covert.
"Esther, by your looks,
There 's preaching or exhorting going on,
And I need talking to. What is it, pray?"

"We spoke of work," said Esther.
"Oh! of work!
I 'm wiser on that subject than you all, —
A farmer's daughter, taught to cook and churn

As soon as I could toddle. But, indeed,
I came to agitate this very theme, —
What labor I 'm best fit for. I 'm possessed
By some old Indian's restless ghost, I think.
I long for — what I know not ! — to strike out
For something new, — to learn what 's in me. Work ?
As well as quit living as quit work, and yet
Heads like to be employed, as well as hands ;
Is there no way to give each a fair chance ?"

" Why, yes," said Miriam. " Have you never heard
Of the Brook Farm experiment, now being tried ?
A well-born friend of mine was there, for weeks,
Doing her share of menial work, to give
Others free hours for study : and she learned,
In that community, to reverence hands
Hardened by useful toil, no less than brows
Bent with the weight of thought."

" But there 's no home
For any one, in everybody's home ;
And home's the very best of selfish things
In all this selfish world," said Eleanor.
" ' In families He sets the solitary ' ;
' In phalansteries,' Fourier would say.

Esther, and our one little room, is more
To me than ten Brook Farms."

"And, on the whole,
Miss Willoughby, I 'd rather struggle on,
And puzzle out my problem by myself,"
Said Minta; "'t is the simplest thing to do;
I will ask no man's help or blessing. Laugh!
And laugh you will; but I am bound to be
A scholar or a writer, if I can!"

Frowning and smiling in her earnestness,
Fresh from defying Solon the Unwise,
Minta went on:
"If I had but your gifts,
Esther! — for do you know, Miss Willoughby,
She studies History, and German, too,
And Moral Science, somehow, between work;
And — do not mind her threatening shake of head —
She can write prose and poetry; I 've seen both
In the 'Offering,' — you know the magazine
That the girls publish. Esther, I won't tell
Whether you 're 'Blanche' or 'Stella'!
"Evening schools
We have, Miss Willoughby, and I have known

Girls to keep up with their Academy class
By studying on, while earning at the mills
Their graduating dresses; why not I?
I might, perhaps, go to Mount Holyoke School
And work my way through, by and by. We have
Our evenings, seven to ten, — that 's three hours
clear,
For study. And you know a spinner's work,
Esther, is not the kind that pins one close
As yours, a weaver's. There are hours and hours,
When the warp spins well, I just sit and think,
And do sums in my head, build air-castles,
Or take the world to pieces; and I might
Learn the whole algebra and geometry
By snatches, so; and puzzle through the rules
Of Latin Grammar. Now Ruth Woodburn 's there,
Who 'd ask a better teacher?

"I 've a plan,
Esther! Do you and she set up a school,
And take me in, and Eleanor, to assist.
She can do beautiful fine sewing; girls
Ought to be proud to learn of her. And I
Will run the home-department, make the bread,
And teach girls how. We 'll have all ages in,
And show the elder, while they 're growing up,

How to be mothers to the younger. Why,
Esther, I more than half believe I 've found
Old Archimedes' secret! Only now
Give me a money-lever, and I 'll move
The world into a new thought about girls
And schools to train them in.
"Alas! alas!
Instead of money, because names are cheap,
Our parents give us country girls grand names:
Mine, now, is Araminta Summerfield,
Written out, full? But in this school of ours,
We 'll work up to our names or over them.
My hands in dough, my thoughts upon my books,
I 'll come out with you wise ones, in the end."

And Miriam, listening, though amused, was moved
By thoughts new-wakened. On the working-side
She had not stood, with working-girls, before.
She asked herself if she, in girlhood's dawn,
Would have striven through such hindrances, if she
Would not have yielded to despair, and drudged,
And only drudged, her daily fourteen hours, —
Their work-day's length, nor ever touched a book,
Or nursed an aspiration.
Miriam shared

With all New-Englanders an honest pride
In the provincial energy and sense;
But this was waste, — this woman-faculty
Tied to machinery, part of the machine
That wove cloth, when it might be clothing hearts
And minds with queenly raiment. She foresaw
The time must come when mind itself would yield
To the machine, or leave the work to hands
Which were hands only.
Just to think of it!
Minta, so full of health, ability,
And right aspirings; Esther, whom she felt
At least an intellectual equal; and —
This most unfit of all — sweet Eleanor,
A flower of delicate birth and saintly-pure; —
These counted but as "hands!" named such!
No! no!
It must not be at all; or else their toil
Must be made easier, larger its reward!
These girls, too, from their talk, were not so far
Above the rest. Here was a problem, then,
For the political theorist: how to save
Mind from machinery's clutches. And, meanwhile,
She would help out of their entanglements,
Into such freedom as she could, these girls.

Jogging on with the white horse, by this time
They reached the Inn. Strangers about the door
Were loitering as they entered. "Can it be?"
Eleanor whispered. "It is Doctor Mann!"
He grasped her hand. "Now," Minta said, aside,
To Esther, roguishly, "I 'll only take
You home with me, although I came for both."
But Miriam overheard, just bringing up
Another new-arrived, her nephew Ralph.
"Not one goes back to-night! Wizard and all
Must stay; to-morrow will be time enough,
And better time than this."

She had her way,
Esther demurring, for to her it seemed
As if Fate's messenger had surely come,
Shaped as a young physician, to bear off
Her more than sister, Eleanor. Shutting back
Her jealous thoughts, she joined the company
Around the maple-blaze on the wide hearth,
And heard these guests retrace their journeyings.

The young physician had been following up
The Pemigewasset's windings, and had seen
A sunrise from the fields of Bethlehem,
A sunset on the Saco meadows; while

The stranger, Ralph, had travelled from the east
Among gigantic mountain-majesties
Skirting the Androscoggin. They had met
Under Moat Mountain's shadow; had grown friends
Tossing together in the stage-coach, through
Oak-barren sands, from Conway to the Inn;
And, like two meeting streams, they seemed to bring
Freshness of unimagined distances
About the little group, where laughter rose,
Rippled, and billowed, only eddying down
At some long repetition of the hour
From the old timepiece underneath the stairs.
Hearing which warning, one by one dropped out,
Till Miriam and her nephew Ralph were left
Alone beside the smouldering ember-glow.

XI.

Up through the morning mist a horseman came,
Before the guests were stirring at the Inn,
Save Minta, who ran down the hill to meet
Her brother, recognized far off.
"See here!
A letter! 't is for Esther, marked 'In haste!'
I hurried over with it."
Haste, indeed!
It was Ruth's hand, and but a word or two:
"Esther, come back! on Isabel's account.
Leave Eleanor with Minta, if you can!"
No more. But Esther felt a heavy weight
Of fear condensed therein, and told her dread
To Miriam Willoughby, while yet asleep
Lay Eleanor. "Leave her here with me," she said,
"And go with Minta and her brother. I
Will soften your departure. Dear! I love
Eleanor well as you do."

With a pang
Of inward protest, Esther heard, but thanked
Her friend, and turned away. And ere the sun
Had passed meridian, Clement Summerfield
Stood with her at the lake-side, where the boat,
Puffing and panting, waited. Passengers
Were crossing to the deck. Farewells were said.
Esther, absorbed and lonely, stepped on board,
When some one called her name.
"Why, Doctor Mann!
I thought you meant to stay awhile. I thought,
With Eleanor there —"
What was she speaking of?
She stopped herself, and added: "Eleanor
I had to leave behind; and so was glad —
She is so delicate — that you would stay;
Her friend, and a physician."
"But indeed
She sent me word — she had not left her room
When the coach started — to look after you,
As you might need my help. I pray you then,
If trouble should be," — and her anxious face
Revealed its presence plainly, — "take my aid,
Just as you would a brother's."
"And I will,"

Responded Esther, for a brother's name
Was dearer than all others to her dreams;
And then, if Eleanor cared for Doctor Mann,
As he for her, as everybody must —
To know her was to love her — by and by,
Perhaps — but there she broke her musings off
At her companion's voice, recalling her
To the fair vision of receding hills,
Now known as friends. She named them, one by one,
Black Mountain, Whiteface, Passaconaway;
And their snow patches seemed like kerchiefs waved
After her from afar. Chocorua,
Bending his crown of pearl, almost drew tears
Into her eyes: "He guards my Eleanor,"
Her heart said, with a grateful homesickness.

No railway-whistle then its discords mixed
With echoes of the hills; and they must wait
The morning stage-coach. Esther would have given
Worlds for the legendary tapestry
Of the Arabian Nights, to travel on
Without delay; and grudged the lovely hours
Of harvest-moonlight on the tinted woods
And dark pine-islands; the blue, rippling lake

Seemed whispering low forebodings and regrets;
And she was glad, upon the morrow morn,
Of every lumbering jolt that hurried her
On through her journey.
Wayside travellers
Dropped in and out again; among them, two
Who roused her from her anxious reveries, —
A prettily dressed girl, with wandering eyes,
And movements of the studied picturesque,
Followed by an unwilling squire, who bore
Shawls and umbrellas, and appealing looks,
Petulant or pathetic, with the same
Tired, uninterested air. "Bride or betrothed,"
Thought Esther, "she is baggage all the same,
Which he would gladly drop." The stranger talked
With Doctor Mann, talked well. The beauty sat
Pouting beside him, trying now and then
To attract both from dull topics to herself,
Sometimes successfully; then her eyes shone
Through all their shallows; voluble nonsense poured
From her bright lips, while her companion blushed.

They left the coach, and Esther heard her say,
In tones most unendearing, "Ambrose, dear!"
Thinking herself unheard. The name flashed back

Ruth's story on her memory. This was he
Through whose desertion shipwreck had wellnigh
Come to her friend! She almost pitied him,
False as he was. With that vexatious bark
Always in tow, what harbor could he gain?
Were this indeed his bride, Ruth was avenged
In his ridiculously hopeless fate.

At last the travellers heard the river rush
Over the rocks at Amoskeag; and close
Winding along the widening Merrimack,
As the coach rumbled on, the Doctor told
Strange Western stories. Prairie-grasses waved,
And great lakes glistened through his talk; mounds rose,
Wondrous with handiwork of tribes unknown:
The fading trail of tawny races died
Along the Mississippi's turbid sweep,
And over white sierras, into haze
Of the Pacific. New horizons grew
On Esther's thought, and almost a surprise
Came to her, in the line of factory-lights
Shimmering up from the river to the stars,
Lengths of reflected jewels.

At the door

Opening familiar in the long brick row,
Ruth met her, smileless.
"Where is Isabel?"

"O Esther, hush! I know not."
Doctor Mann
Saw fear dissolve in anguish on the face
Of Esther Hale, and hastened, without pause,
To Pastor Alwyn.
Meanwhile, everything
Ruth had to tell was of the Monday past,
When Isabel, for a headache, left her work,
And never had returned; had taken all
Her little wardrobe, too.
Looking far back,
The two girls called up memories now, which meant
Much pain, as fear translated them; and blame
Took Esther to herself for hints let slip:
And, self-reproved for all the happy days
Spent out of sight of Isabel, she said,
"Whoever dares to entertain a joy
Does it at risk of letting sorrow in,
And a whole rabble of regrets. My fault
It is, my fault! my poor lost Isabel!
I should have stayed with her, and I must go
To the ends of the earth to find her."

Now there came
A timid rap; two little girls peeped in:
"We saw her go, — that pretty Isabel, —
We saw her in a chaise; a gentleman
Was driving fast. 'T was up the Boston road,
Where they are building the great railway-arch;
And Ann and I were gathering ferns and leaves
To trim the grammar-school room, where we 've been
All summer, for examination-day.
The gentleman got out to fix the reins
And then drove off quick; but he dropped this card."
And Alice laid in Esther's hand the name
Of Rodney Willoughby.
"Why, Ruth! why, Ruth!
The very name of our dear lady-friend
Up under Ossipee Mountains, where I left
Our Eleanor! Scarcely could kin of hers
A villain be; but this may prove a clew."

The little messengers had slipped away,
And now came Pastor Alwyn.
All being told,
He said: "Take heart! Give me this card, and soon
Tidings will come to you. Do not despair
Of her who wanders! followed by our prayers,

And by the All-Loving Heart, she must be saved" :—
Divulging not who waited to depart
In quest of Isabel.

The sleepless night
Passed by at last, and Esther said to Ruth :
"To stay here is impossible ; I must track
Isabel's footsteps. While a penny lasts
I 'll spend it looking for her. 'T is the fault
Of my self-confidence, if she has strayed.
I never thought a girl could be beguiled
Easily as men say. Beauty like hers
Is its own dreadful snare, I learn too late.
No ! not too late ! It shall not be too late !"

Before the day closed Esther found herself
Sheltered in Boston, underneath the roof
Of a kind work-mate's mother, an old house
Which had seen better days, though now reduced
To a cheap lodging-place for sewing-girls,
Shop-tenders, tailoresses, milliners ;—
A tall, quaint building of Colonial date,
Upon the western slope of Beacon Hill,
In an irregular street, where clean-patched clothes
And stiff brocades found jostling neighborhood.

The chat of the house-inmates wearied much
The soul of Esther, — idle prattle, all
Of fashions, scandal, good looks, stylish beaux:
She wondered at it greatly; used, herself,
To talk that held some meaning. Could it be
That much toil on the outside shows of things
Deadened the deeper faculties? Her room
Became the refuge of her restless heart,
High in the attic-eaves, whence she could look
Over the city; and, in wakefulness,
She watched the twinkling lights that went and came,
Blooming and fading out like golden flowers
In gardens of the Night. Souls of her dead,
Mother, friends, sisters, in that starry hush
Appeared, and disappeared, and reappeared
Through memory's dusk. The mystery of Death
Had approached Esther in her earliest years.
Familiar with his lineaments undefined,
Ever a friendly Awe seemed waiting near,
Under whose shadowy cloak her best-beloved
Were shielded from earth's harm.

Extinguished light,
She could not think one heart's love had become
Which had enkindled steady flame in hers,
Flame that illumed the untrodden wilderness

Of the Unknown, the vast Beyond of life.
This was her heart's unburdening in such hours: —

THE CITY LIGHTS.

UNDERNEATH the stars the houses are awake;
Upward comes no sound my silent watch to break.
Night has hid the street, with all its motley sights;
Miles around, afar, shine out the city lights.

Stars that softly glimmer in a lower sky,
Dearer than the glories unexplored on high;
Home-stars, that, like eyes, are glistening through the dark,
With a human tremor wavers every spark.

Glittering lamps above and twinkling lamps below;
The remote, strange splendor, the familiar glow, —
One Eye, looking downward from creation's dome,
Sees in both his children's window-lights of home.

Who have dwellings there, in avenues of space?
Whose clear torches kindle through the vague sky-place?

Are they holding tapers, us, astray, to guide, —
Spirit-pioneers, who lately left our side?

Never drops an answer from those worlds unknown.
Yet no ray is shining for itself alone.
Hints of Heaven gleam upward, through our earthly
nights;
Tremulous with pathos are the city lights: —

Tremulous with pathos of a half-told tale:
Though therein hope flickers, burning low and pale,
It shall win completeness perfect as the sun:
Broken rays shall mingle, earth and heaven be one.

But every hour of daylight Esther spent
Searching hotel-books and stage-offices;
Met, oftentimes, by insult or rebuff:
She cared not. And through streets unfrequented
By maid or matron, she went, sorrowful,
Undaunted by coarse look or muttered sneer
Of masculine unmanliness. She saw
Vanishing in blind alleys, through dim doors,
Faces that thrilled her with a horrible hint
Of likeness to the wanderer. Womanhood,

Sunk to its lowest, scoffed at the pure eyes
Looking with questioning pity into theirs;
For the dark secret of their straying still
Bewildered Esther, and the atmosphere
Poisoned her, with its stench of unclean souls.
Daily her heart grew humbler, at the sight
Of misery and despair; her ignorance
Of life's bad possibilities appalled her. "This,
This is the second death!" she said, "and these
Are spirits in prison! What deeper hell can be?"

O, what relief, after a day like this,
To snatch from one hour's sleep a heavenly dream
Of the clear mountain-heights and Eleanor!

And one day, watching an arriving coach
With anxious eagerness, lo! Eleanor!
And Miriam Willoughby, and a man, — yes, Ralph,
Lifting out Eleanor! The face beloved
Was paler than its wont. With words of joy
Broken by sobbing questions, Esther caught
Her darling's hand.

"Esther, control yourself!"
Said Miriam, gently. Strange that such reproof
Esther, the staid, sedate, should need! Her will

Had borne her over-wearied heart too long,
Which cried out, as a babe a nurse lets fall.
"Esther, control yourself! for she is ill,
Our Eleanor. Here must we rest to-night.
Stay with us! We have much to tell and hear!"

But Esther, entering, glanced back, and saw
A beckoning eye. "Miss, if you please!" one said,
In tones respectful, reaching out to her
A paper slip. "News of the wanderer;
Good news!" — no more; in handwriting unknown.

Back Esther's self-reliance surged. She kissed
Eleanor, resting in a quiet room;
Promised Miss Willoughby to come to her
To-morrow, in her quiet country-seat,
Westward, beyond the Charles, and then returned
To her own lodging. A note waited her
In the same unknown hand. "In such a street,
At such a number, look for her you seek."

She found the place, well kept, respectable,
A dining-room with girl-attendants. She,
Seating herself, yet veiled, saw one approach,
Let her come close, then took her hand, and said,

"Isabel!" softly. Isabel would have fled,
But that a warm grasp held her, close as heaven's;
She dropped into a chair, pale, still as death.

Esther said, "Isabel, come! go home with me!"
She whispered back, "But you must hear me, first."
And, asking leave, withdrew with her. The two
Paced the long gravel-paths beneath the elms
Of Boston Common, while the gold leaves blew
About them, in the chilly sunset-light.

Isabel's sorrow, her pent-up remorse,
Burst through its flood-gates now.

"I 've been a fool
Esther, a fool! unworthy of such love
As yours, — yet not so wicked as I seem;
Though I deceived you, and deceived the man
Who has forsaken me. We never met
Except on Sundays, between services;
Never but once, last April, by the Falls
He passed me, following some friends of his;
But loitered with his silly flatteries
Till Eleanor came in sight. Those Sunday noons
You used to think me lingering with the girls,

I walked with him, but never let him come
Near the mills with me. Telling half the truth,
I wove romances for him. He believed
I was an orphan seamstress, who was born
To wealth and luxury. Of my factory life
I never hinted, thinking by and by
To be his lady-bride, and, far away,
Lose every memory of my working days.

"I thought I loved him; and he said enough
Of loving me at first sight, and all that,
To turn my silly head; then suddenly,
In a five-minutes' talk, the Sunday noon
Before I came away, said all was planned:
We to be wedded the next day; his ship
To sail on Tuesday; business hurrying him
Out of the country. On his grand estates
I should live like a princess. Time to think
He would not give me. Here we drove, post-haste.
He left me, on arriving at an inn,
Bonneted, waiting his return. Since then
I have not seen him. That some accident
Kept him, I feared. But the landlady laughed
At such a hint, with knowing looks. My tears
Awoke her pity, and she found me work.

It was so dreadful, that uncertainty,
Waiting for him I trusted, all whose words
Had sounded honorable, — left alone
And penniless, — life looked so black with fears!
Yet I must live, — I would earn honest bread;
I begged for any drudgery.
"Back to you
I was ashamed to come. But O the hard,
The hideous whispers men and women, too,
Have made me listen to, have meant for me!
I have risked my good name! What shall I do?
You all must hate me! Eleanor I 've killed,
Perhaps. I wish I could but kill myself! —
And yet, except in wanderings of my heart,
I am an innocent girl."
It was not strange
That, next day, under Miriam Willoughby's roof
Isabel found a refuge. It was like
Her Christian, womanly heart, — this Miriam,
Who called not anything she had her own,
Not even the stones of her ancestral hearth,
That echoed proud traditions. Human need,
With her, drowned out aristocratic claims,
And under her calm, helpful eyes, these girls
Sat down to look new futures in the face.

She was not spared her pang. A message came
From Ralph, returned to business. "Dearest aunt,
Rodney has disappeared. Embezzlements
Are known. They must be his. He has escaped
Arrest, and I shall cover his disgrace
By payment. Doubtless he has crossed the sea."

The criminal was her nephew! All the more
Would Miriam shield the girl whom he had left
Exposed to ruin. Yet she could but feel
How the great body of humanity
Shares every member's stain. One loss
The misery, meanness, and disease! One hope
Breaking through heavenly vistas on mankind!

Isabel's hands were deft, and work for them
Found Miriam; kept her at white sewing-work
By Eleanor's bedside, who had rallied now,
Though restless with the wanderer out of sight;
So restless, Isabel said, through tears and smiles, —

"You are severe with me as Sister Sterne, —
The blessed, cross old thing! Upon my knees
I 'd fall before her, if I could! I know
She always meant my good. You both are saints,

Though so unlike; saintly antipodes.
O Eleanor, I laugh, when I should weep!
But will you never trust me, never more?"

For Isabel would not stray again. Her life
Bared now its firm foundations, overgrown
Before with falsehoods, that she pruned away
As she perceived them; and so beautiful
She grew, self-conquering, strangers, seeing her,
Wondered about her, as at fairy tales.

But Isabel now beheld not her own face
With any pleasure. From her glass a ghost,
Refusing to be laid, looked out at her
With her own eyes,—such as hers might have been,
Hope's light extinguished, pure tears burned away.
If Rodney Willoughby had truly meant
What he had promised, she had walked ashamed
Beside him, as a banished felon's wife,
Arrayed in thievery's spoil. With that vile fate
Compared, a menial's lot were Paradise.

Esther watched Eleanor's pale loveliness,
And marvelled at it, too. If Doctor Mann
Could see her now! Thinking of him, she said:
"Once, Eleanor, I liked not this your friend.

He seemed to patronize us working-girls,
As some strange, pitiable phenomena, —
Lusus naturæ to all well-bred folk.

But either I mistook him, or he found
Himself mistaken; for more deferent
Or manlier courtesy never have I met,
Nor wiser thinking listened to than his.
On your account I should dislike him still,
For I believe he loves you. But I 've grown
Magnanimous. God bless him!"

A strange look,
A far-off smile, came into Eleanor's eyes:
"Esther, — yes, he is good. But do you know,
I have a lovely secret of my own,
And I shall wed another. By and by
I 'll tell you all about it."

That same night
Came the young Doctor, with kind messages
From Pastor Alwyn; spent a brief half-hour
In low, calm talk with Eleanor alone, —
For Eleanor loved him with a cousinly trust,
And she to him was like own kith and kin;
Truly his cousin, by a few removes, —
Then asked for Esther Hale.

The house was hushed
When he departed; not so Esther's heart,
Astonished at itself and at his words,
Disturbed with a new presence, hopes and fears
Never before admitted. All the while
It had been Esther his soul bowed before, —
Her warm heart, her illumining intellect,
Her charity, blent with stainless rectitude;
He felt himself grow manlier, loving her.

And in their short acquaintance she had seen
Great depths of an unconscious nobleness
Glimpsed by his words and actions. He it was
Who found out Isabel, Esther kept in sight,
Plunging into foul places for a pearl
Counted as lost.

If now he sought to join
This strong, pure woman's heart to his, to go
Through the sick world beside her, carrying health
And hope, as in an overflowing cup, —
The cup of love the hands of two hold, —
What then? and why not so?

But Esther stood
Dismayed at revelations of herself,
Weak where she had seemed strong, and shrinking back

From visions that reality might spoil.
Disloyalty to Eleanor? to her own
Half-builded plans and purposes? No, no!
She could not choose her own lot. God knew best!
And with this prayer at last she closed her eyes:—

A PRAYER is in my thoughts to-night
 I hardly dare to say:
"Lord, put my wishes all to flight,
 Nor let me have my way!"

I dare not say it, Lord, for fear
 My heart I may mistake;
So many earthly things are dear,
 Perhaps, for earth's own sake.

Nor can I think that thou art glad
 In life despoiled of bloom,
Since for all joy the worlds have had
 Thyself hast opened room.

And yet the poison-plant, so fair,
 So like the wholesome grows,
To pluck my flower I will not dare,
 But trust His hand who knows.

And this, indeed, is life's best thing :
  To take sweet gifts from thee.
If thou some dark, sealed bud shouldst bring,
  It must hold light for me.

In sadness I withheld my prayer,
  Hid under trembling fear ;
In praise it blossoms, unaware,
  Because the sun is near.

My heart thou wilt not crush or chill.
  "Lead into thine my way !
Through all my wishes breathe thy will !"
  This prayer to-night I say.

XII.

An autumn day beside the Merrimack,
Deepening its color betwixt rocky steeps
Dyed rich with crimson oak and purple ash,
And stray flakes of the maple's airier red;
With clouds of asters on the turf, and flames
Of golden-rod just fading out above,
Against cool rocks and sky. Below, three girls
Upon a knoll reclining. Two were fair;
And all three faces frank and lovable.

Far up the bank a merry picnic-group,
In story-telling, sports, and songs, forgot
Absence of these three, — Esther, Minta, Ruth.
Together once more for a little while,
They talked as girls do, by themselves; and turned
Thoughts, wishes, troubles, inside out. Each laughed
At each, — sweet, loving laughter; now and then
Almost pathetic, for it held farewells.

Changes had come. Hope's pretty cob-houses
Fate had demolished; Minta so complained.
That Esther Hale should form a partnership
With Doctor Archibald Mann, and emigrate,
As now seemed likely, — that was hard to bear;
But Ruth to leave her also, — 't was too much!

Where was Ruth going? A rich lady friend
Of Miriam Willoughby's, soon to cross the sea
With growing daughters, for long residence,
A teacher sought; and Eleanor made Ruth known,
Her gifts and her acquirements; these were all
The lady asked, who gladly gave, in turn,
Thrice the mill-fees. The one enthusiasm
Of Ruth was study of the Old-World ways,
Languages, histories. She surprised herself
With eager, girlish freshness of delight
She never had expected. Lives like hers
Get cheated out of youth sometimes; but now
Minta seemed scarcely younger: and indeed,
Minta was grave to-day; though, for all that,
Her eyes laughed — they did always — while she drew
Pictures of Esther as the Doctor's wife
Visiting ague-patients at his side
Out in the unknown Somewhere of the West: —

"You, firmest old maid of us all! Just think!
You, who have painted single blessedness
So bright, you drew us into league with you
Against mankind and for our liberties;
O Esther, you, of all girls!

"And you, Ruth,
Whom I had counted on to teach me all
I want to know, and more, — you must steer off
Among your countesses and duchesses,
And by and by be one yourself, perhaps;
For stranger things have happened. There 's a girl
I used to know, who went to Mexico
When cotton-mills were built there, and is now
Wife of some ruling officer, and at home
In halls of the Montezumas. That sounds grand,
Although she may not be so comfortable
As in a well-chinked log-house."

"O," said Ruth,
"I take my democratic heart with me,
And mean to bring it back, whole. Rather, far,
I 'd weave cloth here my life long, than lose that!
Woman can climb no higher than womanhood,
Whatever be her title."

"I confess,"
Said Esther, "disappointment at myself,

Dear Minta, — for I meant to honor it,
Blessed old-maidhood! as my chosen lot.
We do not choose; our way is all mapped out
By the unknown Wisdom! No one more surprised
Than I, at my own present happiness!
I never dreamed of aught so beautiful
As life looks now before me.

"The old maid,
Who makes the name disgrace, you cannot be,
Minta, with all your deep unselfishness,
Your glad health, bounding fancy, and light heart.
I think the sweetest women I have known
Have lived on single, happy to the end,
And happiness-creators."

"I 'm consoled!"
Laughed Minta, "and accept the inevitable
With a good grace, since worse was possible, —
You know I might have married Solon Dale!
Now hearken to my plans and theories!
I mean to learn; and then I mean to teach
Girls to be thorough women, wives or maids.
Health of soul, mind, and body, but without
Self-coddling, shall be first; and after that,
All wisdom, all accomplishments desired.
It is my firm faith that the alphabet

Was meant for woman's use as much as man's.
Devotion to it no more injures her
Than sacrifice at stove-and-kitchen shrines,
Or bowing down before the deity
Enthroned on ruffles, plumes, and furbelows.
Neat dress is good, and so is housewifery ;
But there is something in the spelling-book
More valuable than either. Human beings
God made us, then he added womanhood ;
And never does he add to mar his work
Or lower its greatness. An intelligence
Is woman, or a failure."

"Even so!"

Said Ruth; "and presently I shall return
And in your school take my professorship,
Unless a wiser Solon finds you out,
And you slip off, as Esther has."

"Dear girls,"

Joined Esther, "bright have been our working-days
Together; and yet happier times will be
Than all our happiest here. Yes, by and by,
When Ruth returns, you both must come to me,
And at my Western fireside we will read
Our life's continued story.

"Eleanor, too.

What think you? Is it possible that she
And Ralph should love each other? Just a hint
She dropped once, before ever Archibald Mann
Was anything to me more than to her.
And Isabel, — I want her so with me
In my new home! but Miriam Willoughby
Claims her, claims both of them.
"The fairy prince
She used to laugh about may find her yet,
Ere Miriam thinks of it; may come disguised
Like a young carpenter I 've lately seen
Working at Willoughby Place. I 've watched his look
When she has passed; a timid, earnest gaze,
I 've learned to understand. But Isabel
Will not too easily trust any man,
After the dangerous risk she ran with one.
Still, when I overheard her hum these words
The other day, they seemed significant: —

What trade shall with his compete?
What honor can earth confer
Like this, — to be found at the feet
Of the Son of the carpenter?

Around hammer and chisel, the hand
Of Christ leaves a halo grand.

"O Esther! Ruth!" cried Minta; "after all,
'T is work we love, and work we long to do;
But always better work, and better still:
Is not that right ambition? The good God,
Letting us labor, makes us like himself, —
Creator, glad in his accomplished work,
Ever beginning, perfect evermore!"

"If we could work like Him!" said Ruth. "We hold
Our single thread, and that one broken thread
Can make such mischief with the web! I 've seen
One thread drop down through the long films of warp
Winding themselves around the dresser's beam,
And catch, and tangle, and make such a snarl
As hours could not undo. And after all
Mending attempted, with the woof filled in,
'T was marked 'Imperfect'; doomed to some cheap
use."

Then Minta: "And the spinner of that thread, —
I might have been the one, — careless of oil,
Or band, or spindle, was responsible;

Not you who dressed, or she who wove. So back
To their beginnings good and evil go,
One wretched blunder spoiling a whole life;
And yet — we all are blunderers."

"Not quite all;
At least, not so to me. Though some pick flaws
In Pastor Alwyn, through him we have learned
That 'minister' is no unmeaning word.
His character and sermons harmonize,
So winning us to sympathy with truth,
We are led unaware, and all as one,
In search of it. And Miriam Willoughby,
The busiest weaver of us all, — our lives
Have gathered strength beneath her touch; and yet
I 've heard her styled 'lofty aristocrat,'
Because of her fine manners," Esther said.

"And that is what I call vulgarity,"
Cried Minta; "not to know the genuine ring,
Or glimmer of pure gold from counterfeit.
True ladies are true women, poor or rich;
Yet human nature needs to be refined,
Like gold and silver."

"Girls, dear girls," said Ruth,
"You guess not what good work you 've done for me,

Since I have known you! Sentimental, weak,
A baby crying for lost playthings, I
Seem to myself to have been; to say 'am'
I can refuse with honesty, thank Heaven
And you! I 've seen you sacrifice so much
For others, — seen you full of cheerfulness
When I could only mope, I 've been ashamed
Before you, in my thoughts. Why, how absurd
To think, one moment, that a human soul
Was set here just to gratify itself,
However innocently! There 's no loss
For any one of us. God takes away
The things we do not need, and fills our hands
With useful implements, bidding us work out
Our own salvation, and our neighbor's, too;
And nothing else *is* living."

And Ruth's voice
Died softly into reverie, while her heart
Kept time to this inaudible undertone: —

No burden ever had I
  That I would not have had,
Though times there were when I thought never again
  To look up to Heaven and be glad.

For, groaning and struggling on
  With the throngs that laden go,
I saw, by the pack on my neighbor's back,
  That mine was the lighter woe.

Unladen, heedless, unbent,
  I never had known
That the fardel borne by each wight forlorn
  Held something that was my own, —
Something he bore for me
  With a patient ignorance,
While my footsteps lay as a blur on his way,
  And hindered his soul's advance.

Just it was that on me
  Some sorrow should fall;
No trouble alone is the trouble of one,
  But each has a share in all.
And if on my aching neck
  Another his burden laid,
Strength given for his day then he threw away,
  Wherewith I was stronger made.

I know that we are not here
  For our selfish ease;

The kingliest One that the earth has known
  Lived not himself to please.
And they who have learned of him
  How a burden can give rest,
And joyfully share the great human care, —
  They have learned life's secret best.

But now late afternoon had changed to gold
The rippling silver of the Merrimack,
And the gay company, in twos and threes,
Gathered around the girls for parting. This,
A holiday of love and of regret,
A score or two had taken, the intimates
Of one or all.
                Turn forward, leaves of fate!
There 's one will go among the Cherokees,
A mission-teacher. At the Capitol
One will be seen, bride of a Senator.
A country and a city parsonage
Await those grave-eyed sisters. Alice, there,
Will sail with her proud Captain round the globe,
While little Ann paints pictures with her pen.
That broad-browed, delicate girl will carve, at Rome,
Faces in marble, classic as her own.

And this, a millionnaire's wife, will regret
Her dear old factory-nook, and the clear gold
The sunshine coined there, bringing her no care.
Some will wear out in schools their faithful lives;
And most be happy wives, in thrifty homes,
Mothers of men and women.
Like the sea
Must the work-populations ebb and flow,
So only fresh with healthful New-World life.
If high rewards no longer stimulate toil,
And mill-folk settle to a stagnant class,
As in old civilizations, then farewell
To the Republic's hope! What differ we
From other feudalisms? Like ocean-waves
Work-populations change. No rich, no poor,
No learned, and no ignorant class or caste
The true republic tolerates; interfused,
Like the sea's salt, the life of each through all.

In that third decade past, thoughts grave as these
Could scarcely visit the young toiler's mind,
Who knew her labor transient; who at will
Took up or dropped her shuttle, well assured
That life had various need of her two hands.
Mill-work meant then a fresh society

Of eager, active youth, long held apart
In rustic hamlets; that, like flint and steel,
Meeting, struck light from faculties unknown.

And all around, the rough idyllic strength
Of old New England lay; — the morning keen
Upon the sharp-cut hills; the steel-blue sea
Binding the brawny continent, that kept
The secret of its power untold. That hour
Can never be repeated. Whoso toils
To-day toils in a different atmosphere.
The chariot-wheels of Progress fill the air
With dust. — Yes, it was something to be born
While this gray Mother Century was young.

The group dispersed. Good wishes and good byes
Filled the crisp autumn air. The Merrimack
Whispered a parting from its hollow bed;
And, with that nightfall, Ruth and Esther, too,
Beheld the close of their mill-working days.

Not many evenings later, Esther sat
By Eleanor, in her room at Willoughby Place,
That looked across the blue breadth of the Charles

To the old Trimountain City, fading back
In twilight shadow, its gray State House dome
Touched with a dusky crimson from the west,
Where the sun sank, a red, distended orb ; —
Yet stayed, unwilling to lose sight of earth.

Eleanor, reclined in a carved Indian chair,
Leaned back on pillows, white-robed, her soft eyes,
Under dark hair smooth-parted, shining out
From her Madonna forehead ; a pink glow
Like the last tint of sunset in her cheek :
So beautiful, the faces at the door,
Isabel's, Miriam's, ere they disappeared,
Turned back and gazed again. She seemed a part
Of the suffusing harmony of light
In which the world lay tranced ; and Esther looked,
And breathed no word, for fulness of her heart.

But Eleanor spoke at last : —
"Esther, I said
I had a secret, once. Have you not guessed,
By this time, what it is?"
The name of Ralph
Arose through Esther's thoughts, — Ralph, who had sent

Messages, offerings of fruit and flowers
To the sweet invalid often, — Ralph, the one
Whom, of all others, for his tenderness,
His probity, his manhood, she would trust
With her beloved one, now she knew so well
The joy of being loved and loving back.
Ralph, one of the strong souls born to protect,
Might well revivify a drooping life,
Delicate as her friend's; or, failing that,
Beautify its decline. Half musingly
She sighed, —
"O Eleanor, a lovelier bride
Than you I cannot picture."
Eleanor,
With a faint wonder fading from her eyes,
Said softly, —
"I? a bride? Yes, Esther, yes!
And in an unknown country I shall find
Such love! and such a home! You look toward yours
In the far, wonderful West; mine from the East
Dawns on me. There 's a City of whose streets
We 've read together; there my Bridegroom lives.
Land of true health, where no inhabitant
Says ever, 'I am sick.'"
Now Esther, hushed

Before the dissolution of her dream
For Eleanor, — in the blindness of her love,
Painting a double marriage, two in white,
Eleanor, herself; and Pastor Alwyn's voice
Blessing two happy brides, — though Ralph indeed
Loved Eleanor but with far-off reverence,
As seraph might love saint, — wept silently
With bowed head, at the long-evaded truth.

But Eleanor's hand lay on her brow, no pain
Thrilling its flower-like touch : —
"For both of us
'T is but a journey; more life and more love
For both of us."
Still, Esther could not raise
Her tearful eyes, till Eleanor besought :
"Esther, dear sister, look up! let us feel
Together this most lovely close of day, —
This evening, which is like a shutting flower
That opens with the sun!
"I do not die!
I fold my petals for immortal dawn!"

And in that twilight hush God drew their hearts
Indissolubly close. For what is love

But His most perfect weaving, — intertwine
Of the soul's deathless fibres, threading in
Our human lives, one weft with the Divine?

There leave them, looking forth into fair realms
Of untried being; into opening heavens
Radiant with invitation. East and West
Life beckons. Nothing satisfies the soul
But opportunity for nobler work,
And glimpses of illimitable fields.

THE END.

Cambridge: Electrotyped and Printed by Welch, Bigelow, & Co.